SAVING NINE

THE FIGHT AGAINST THE LEFT'S AUDACIOUS PLAN
TO PACK THE SUPREME COURT AND
DESTROY AMERICAN LIBERTY

Senator Mike Lee

CENTER STREET

NASHVILLE • NEW YORK

Center Street
Hachette Book Group
1290 Avenue of the Americas, New York, NY 10104
centerstreet.com
twitter.com/centerstreet

First Trade Paperback Edition: June 2023

Center Street is a division of Hachette Book Group, Inc. The Center Street name and logo are trademarks of Hachette Book Group, Inc.

The publisher is not responsible for websites (or their content) that are not owned by the publisher.

The Hachette Speakers Bureau provides a wide range of authors for speaking events. To find out more, go to hachettespeakersbureau.com or email HachetteSpeakers@hbgusa.com.

Library of Congress Cataloging-in-Publication Data
Names: Lee, Mike, 1971- author.
Title: Saving nine : the fight against the left's audacious plan to pack the Supreme Court and destroy American liberty / Senator Mike Lee.
Description: First edition. | Nashville : Center Street, 2022. | Includes bibliographical references. |
Identifiers: LCCN 2022000023 | ISBN 9781546002208 (hardcover) | ISBN 9781546003113 | ISBN 9781546002352 (ebook)
Subjects: LCSH: United States. Supreme Court. | Judges—Selection and appointment—United States. | Political questions and judicial power—United States. | Judicial independence—United States. | Justice, Administration of—Political aspects—United States. | United States—Politics and government—2021-
Classification: LCC KF8742 .L446 2022 | DDC 347.73/26—dc23/eng/20220204
LC record available at https://lccn.loc.gov/2022000023

ISBNs: 978-1-5460-0220-8 (hardcover); 978-1-5460-0234-5 (trade paperback); 978-1-5460-0235-2 (ebook)

Printed in the United States of America

LSC-C

Printing 1, 2023

To my brother, Tom—a jurist's jurist.

CONTENTS

Introduction

"I have heard that there are some people on the Democratic side who would like to increase the number of judges. I think that was a bad idea when President Franklin Delano Roosevelt tried to pack the court."

—Justice Ruth Bader Ginsburg

W HEN THE LATE JUSTICE RUTH BADER GINSBURG made that comment in an interview in 2019, it wasn't particularly controversial. But by the next year, those comments would have placed this particular liberal icon at odds with many—in fact most—of her ideological pals. In 2020, we lost Justice Ginsburg, and many Democrats began to lose their minds. That year on the campaign trail, Joe Biden, the Democratic presidential nominee, refused on many occasions to rule out packing the Court. Other members of his party said the Supreme Court was "broken" and "actively dismantling our democracy." As president, Biden appointed a committee to examine "reforms" to the Court, which signaled to many that he was inclined to support the drastic "reform" of Court packing. When that commission published its report in

2021, it avoided making any concrete recommendations, but it subtly advanced the cause by refusing to condemn expanding the Court in the future. Voices on the Left in and out of government quickly took up the mantle of Court expansion.

How did things change so quickly? Through the course of this book, I'm going to explore this question, and hopefully provide a defense for a nine-justice Court. I hope as well to outline the dangerous norm-shattering precedent that would be set by politically motivated attempts to turn the Supreme Court into just another partisan weapon.

For the last few decades, the American Left and Right have been able to stay in almost complete agreement on very few issues. One of these is the size of the Supreme Court. The nation's highest court has been composed of nine justices since 1869, and that number remained undisturbed until 1937, when Franklin Roosevelt threatened to add more justices to get his New Deal agenda approved. Though Roosevelt did not end up expanding the Court, his threat to do so may have worked just as well: the justices suddenly began to look more favorably on the next New Deal case that came before them.

That seemed to put the matter to rest. For the rest of the twentieth century, Democrats and Republicans left the size of the Supreme Court alone. In 1983, Senator Joe Biden, reflecting on Roosevelt's gambit, called it "a bonehead idea," and "a terrible, terrible mistake to make" that called into question the independence of the nation's highest court.[1] And yet, in 2020, court packing (or court expansion, depending on your side of the issue) became a major election issue, with Biden, then the Democratic nominee, repeatedly coming under pressure to take a firm stance on the question. He managed to come to office without ever detailing his position. But as president, he appointed an entire commission to look into the idea he had once dismissed as "bonehead," reflecting the traction it was gaining within his party.

There are still some serious-minded liberals who have reservations, and aren't afraid to express them. In April 2021, Associate Justice Stephen Breyer told an audience at Harvard that Democrats should think "long and hard" about changes to the Court that would play into the perception that politics played a greater role in their decisions, arguing this would damage public trust in the institution. "Structural alteration motivated by the perception of political influence can only feed that perception, further eroding that trust," he said.[2]

Personally, I agree completely, especially at a time when trust in public institutions is already dangerously low. But it can hardly be a coincidence that progressives were, around the same time, launching a vociferous "Breyer Retire" campaign to force the eighty-two-year-old Bill Clinton appointee off the bench. They had no use for his measured thinking. Eventually, the pressure must have weighed on him: on January 27, 2021, Breyer announced that he would in fact retire. My friend and Democratic colleague in the Senate, Dick Durbin of Illinois, revealed that Biden's chief of Staff, Ron Klain, had leaked the information the day before, when it was widely reported in the press.[3] It is fair to wonder if pressure from the Left on the White House led them to force Breyer's hand.

The progressives on the far-left wing of the Democratic Party are the real drivers behind this issue. Their view was articulated in a video released by freshman New York representative Mondaire Jones, which should horrify anyone, of any political persuasion, who believes in our constitutional system of government. In it, a member of one branch of that government maliciously attacks everything about another branch. Representative Jones maligns not only certain decisions or certain justices he disagrees with, but the entire institution of the Supreme Court itself.

Representative Jones's video shows videos of the January 6, 2021, attack on the Capitol, and he declares: "The Supreme Court helped bring us here," associating the highest court in the land with violence. He goes on to say, "The Court has been actively dismantling our democracy for years." He claims the Court "helped install Donald Trump in the White House," which doesn't line up with any account of the 2016 election that I'm aware of. According to Representative Jones, the institution of the Supreme Court, as it exists today, holds a "far-right, anti-democratic grip on our democracy."[4] The only solution, in his view, is to expand it.

It would be one thing if Representative Jones were an isolated firebrand. The House always has a few of those. But Representative Jerrold Nadler, the House Judiciary Committee chairman, got on board as well. Many of my Democratic colleagues in the Senate got in on the act, especially after a landmark case offered a serious challenge to *Roe* v. *Wade*. Senator Elizabeth Warren, a onetime presidential contender, declared that "the current court threatens the democratic foundations of our nation."[5] Senator Ed Markey said, "the United States Supreme Court is broken," and "out of balance" and "needs to be fixed."[6] In December 2021, *The Washington Post* interviewed "more than a third" of the Senate Democratic Caucus and found a "growing faction" now open to ideas like abolishing lifetime appointments for justices and expanding the Court.[7] The warnings of Ginsburg, Breyer, and even Biden were forgotten. This idea had fully migrated from the fringes into the mainstream.

But why now? Part of it, I believe, is a reaction to the ascendancy over the last few decades of "textualists" and "originalists"—jurists who make it their mission to pay careful heed to the text and original understanding of the law and Constitution—in the federal judiciary. Justice Elena Kagan even acknowledged that this had become the prevailing view in 2015, declaring: "We're all textualists now."[8] A Democratic president adding three non-textualist judges, those who prefer to think of the Constitution as a "living document," could single-handedly undo this favorable development in American jurisprudence.

That would be a general effect. More specifically, an expanded Supreme Court would remove the judiciary's status as the last non-political branch of the federal government. Yes, Democrats would use a biased Court to ram through a liberal wish list in the short term. But such a dramatic move by Democrats would doubtlessly lead Republicans, when they next gain power, to escalate, perhaps adding three more justices. The Court could then grow bigger and bigger, turning into a political football, with its decisions reflecting only the priorities of the party in power rather than text, precedent, and prudence—just what Justice Breyer has warned against. "Landmark" cases would be decided and overturned, and then decided again every few years following each major electoral shift removing consistency and stability from our legal system. That consistency and stability are what give our system its reputation as the best in the world, free from political influence— a reputation that has serious implications for the nation's wider cultural and economic vitality. But if all roads in the federal judiciary lead to a political rubber-stamp Court—for either party—that reputation would erode and eventually disappear.

The way to stop this from happening is to maintain the 150-year precedent and, just as in 1937, "save nine."

CHAPTER ONE

What the Supreme Court Is—and Isn't

E ARLY IN THE SPRING OF 1981, WHEN I WAS TEN YEARS old, I made my way toward the massive front door of the United States Supreme Court for the first time.

My parents, who'd allowed me to take the rare day away from school for the occasion, had briefed me on what to expect during my first visit to the Court. I was expected to sit up straight, remain attentive until the argument session had come to an end, not to fidget, lest I disrupt the proceedings. I'm sure they didn't mean to scare me, but by the time we got in the car to make the short journey to the Court, I was convinced that I'd be arrested immediately by the Supreme Court police if I so much as sneezed while the Court was in session. Perhaps realizing I'd be more likely to focus on the game if I knew the names of the players, they gave me a small piece of paper showing which justice sat in which seat.

Although we entered the Supreme Court through the garage that day, I found myself wishing we had come in through the west entrance after climbing the 44 marble steps that separate the Court from the ground. Even to a ten-year-old kid, even the idea of walking up those steps conveyed some semblance (however faint at the time) of a deeper meaning. It has since occurred to me, that when climbing those stairs, you find yourself leaving the swamp of Washington (and the often-petty political conflicts that abound there) behind, and entering a higher plane of existence.

Which, of course, we were.

Both inside the Court and out, I saw so many important symbols that I hardly knew where to look. On what seemed like every wall, I saw figures that I thought I recognized from school but couldn't quite place. On the outside (just above the west entrance), carved in white marble, was a scene with dozens of historical characters all crowded together. Under them, written in clear block letters, were the words "EQUAL JUSTICE UNDER LAW."

I'm sure I could have spent hours looking at all those statues, friezes, carvings and other artistic depictions of things I knew were significant, even if I couldn't identify them by name. But we didn't have time. We were ushered into a small office, just outside the courtroom, where we waited quietly for a few minutes. At the appointed hour, my mother let us know that it would soon be ten o'clock, when oral arguments before the Court were scheduled to begin.

And as my parents had made sure I knew, the Supreme Court *always* begins on time.

We made the short walk down the hall to the courtroom, walking slowly through the crowd to take our seats near the middle of the room. I again looked around doing my best to process everything I saw. The chamber's main feature was a massive, simple wooden bench with nine empty leather chairs behind it. There was a lectern in the middle of the room, and two long wooden tables on either side.

Each table, I noticed, had a large quill pen and ink placed in the middle.

Even then, the writing implements seemed strange. I knew that down in the real world—the one we had left when we entered the Supreme Court—people didn't use feather pens anymore; in fact, I wasn't sure I had ever even seen one used in real life. But here, in this vaunted chamber, it seemed that they did. The rest of the room, with its old-fashioned depictions of gods and angels, only heightened the impression of being somehow out of time, and maybe even out of this world.

Then, through a small crowd of young men at the front of the room, I saw the familiar face of my father, Rex Lee. He stood at one of those long wooden tables facing the bench, looking over his papers and speaking with some of the lawyers who'd gathered around him. After we had found our seats, he looked at us, waved, and smiled. I could tell that whatever he was about to do, it was something of tremendous importance, both for him and for everyone else in the room.

A few months earlier, shortly after Ronald Reagan defeated Jimmy Carter to become president, my father had been nominated and (following Senate confirmation) appointed by President Reagan as the solicitor general of the United States. As he had explained it to me and my siblings at the dinner table, this meant that he was, effectively, the lawyer for the executive branch of the United States government. Whenever the Reagan administration made an appearance before the Supreme Court, it did so through my father, who would arguing the government's case, attempting in each instance to persuade the Court that the administration's position was correct. If it sounded like a big job, he assured us, that's because it was.

In the early 1980s, the United States was in the midst of a political revolution—one that had been a long time coming. Under the economic policies of President Jimmy Carter, the rate of inflation had remained steadily above 13 percent.[1] Gas prices were soaring, while wages remained stagnant. Even according to liberal politicians like Ted Kennedy, these problems stemmed from "a failure of leadership at the very top."[2] In President Reagan, who had promised "a return to spiritual and moral values" on the campaign trail, voters had found hope, something that was sorely needed at the time.[3]

For years, the American people had watched as the major institutions of this country, particularly the United States Supreme Court, had drifted steadily leftward. Throughout the 1960s and '70s, the Court had issued landmark rulings such as *Roe* v. *Wade*, which, in the view of many prominent legal experts—my father and two dissenting justices of the Supreme Court among them—veered far off course while purporting to the words of the United States Constitution.

On its face, *Roe* v. *Wade* had been simple. The Supreme Court had heard the case of a woman from Texas who wanted an abortion but couldn't get one. At the time, there was a state law in Texas (and many other states) that outlawed abortion except in the most serious of cases. The woman's lawyers wanted the Supreme Court to declare that the Texas state law—and, by extension, all other state laws outlawing the procedure—violated the Constitution, which it clearly did not. Texas had passed a law outlawing abortion, an issue that does not appear in the Constitution. It was all perfectly legal.

But there had been mounting political pressure from activist groups to make abortion legal everywhere, all at once. Given that this was a power that the Constitution rightfully reserved to the states, they couldn't get it all done at once. So they began to pressure the Supreme Court to act in spite of the fact that it had no authority to do so.

Sadly, it worked. In January of 1973, the Court ruled (by a margin of 7–2) to strike down nearly all state laws meaningfully restricting abortion. In the majority opinion, written by Associate Justice Harry Blackmun, the Court declared that government action stopping a woman from getting an abortion would amount to a violation of her right to "due process" under the Fourteenth Amendment—effectively inventing a "right" out of thin air. It was an egregious example of the Supreme Court caving to political pressure from outside the courtroom—something that is supposed to be forbidden. In making its decision, a seven-justice majority had also shown a willingness to treat the Constitution as a so-called "living document," the meaning of which—according to a theory that was gaining traction at the time—should unfold according to "the evolving standards of decency that mark the progress of a maturing society."[4]

This was an approach that my father, along with many princi-
pled legal minds of the era, would spend much of his career trying
to fight. During my dad's time in the Reagan administration, the
Justice Department argued its positions according to what the
Constitution says, regardless of what they or others *wished* it said.
They also took their positions without considering whatever bitter political fights were going on outside the courtroom.

I don't remember which of his many cases my father was
arguing that morning. I'm not even sure whether he, as a representative of the government, was the petitioner (challenging
the lower court's ruling) or the respondent (supporting the
lower court's ruling). Yet there are certain sights and sounds
from that first visit that left an indelible impression on me. To
this day, I can recall them with stunning clarity.

I'm not sure I'll ever forget, for instance, the way the room
suddenly went dead silent at precisely ten o'clock, when the
Court's business was set to begin. If my father had leaned over
and tapped his quill pen on the table in front of him, I would
have been able to hear it from my seat.

I sat, waiting for whatever was about to happen.

Then, no more than a few seconds after ten o'clock, the
silence was broken as the marshal of the Court stepped forward. For years, the marshal has led a kind of security force in
the building, one that works for the justices themselves rather
than any government agency. It is a solemn job that involves
standing guard during oral arguments, deciding who can and
can't come into the building, and, occasionally, removing people.

That morning, in a clear and booming voice, the marshal spoke the incantation that has begun the Court's proceedings since the first time it met in the late eighteenth century.

To this day, I can still recite it from memory.

"The honorable Chief Justice and Associate Justices of the Supreme Court," he said, the sound filling the room, echoing off the white marble and dark wood. At that exact moment, the nine black-robed justices of the Supreme Court, led at that time by Chief Justice Warren Burger, appeared from behind the black velvet curtain in groups of three. The marshal continued the invocation as they made their way to their seats.

"Oyez, Oyez, Oyez!" he said. "All persons having business before the honorable Supreme Court of the United States are admonished to draw near and give their attention, for the Court is now sitting. God save the United States and this honorable Court."

From where I was sitting, the whole thing seemed magical. It was almost as if these nine justices had been summoned into being by the sound of marshal's words, called down to the world of mere mortals from some distant land beyond the curtain.

I was entranced.

For a few minutes, Chief Justice Warren Burger and the others conducted the daily business of the Court. They went over routine motions, most of which involved new lawyers being admitted to the bar. One after another, men and women in suits would approach the bench, state the names of the lawyers whose admission they sought, and then recede. These petitions were all granted, as was (and still is) customary. Then the newly admitted lawyers took their oaths of office, which took about three minutes, and sat back down in a special section off to the side.

After that, the Court wasted no time in getting down to business. The cases were announced, and the petitioners were invited to begin their oral arguments.

It is here, of course, that my memory of that particular morning gets a little foggy—not only because I was ten years old at the time, but because it runs together in my mind with the dozens of other mornings that I spent doing exactly the same thing.

During the years that my father spent as the solicitor general, my family and I attended many of his oral arguments. We watched him argue cases about everything from the right to religious liberty, to the proper role of the federal government in civilian life, to the freedom of speech. We also heard him make the government's case when it came to matters of minute statutory interpretation, attempting to argue the finer points of a very narrow section of a particular clause of a government regulation. (Cases like these, in truth, make up a vast majority of the Court's business during a given year, and they are some of the most fascinating, especially when you've studied the stories and precedent behind them.)

But my father's work was not confined to the grand chamber of the Supreme Court. Even when he was in private practice, it never had been. For as long as I had been alive, my father had brought his work home with him, reading briefs and old opinions in his study and nearly every other room of the house. During family dinners, he would discuss the intricacies of constitutional law with me and any of my siblings who expressed even the slightest interest. We would talk about state statutes and lines of argument. He would hold forth for as long as any of us would listen regarding the implications of a particular federal law. Looking back, I wish I could say that I always paid as much attention as I should have. And I wish I could say that I understood everything he explained about his work. I didn't. But to the extent I did, it was an edifying experience, and instilled in me a love of the law and a reverence for the Constitution that has been with me ever since.

Today, I am a United States Senator for the state of Utah. My brother currently serves as Associate Chief Justice on the Utah Supreme Court, the five-member tribunal that is the court of last resort in my state. I don't get many chances to visit the U.S. Supreme Court these days, being busy with my own work in the legislative branch, but whenever I do, I am reminded of the awe that I felt on that first morning. During one memorable occasion when my brother and I handled a case together in that Court, that feeling nearly overcame me. And it has not dissipated in the years since. If anything, it has only gotten stronger as I have learned more about the law and the Constitution.

Unfortunately, not everyone feels the same way. Given the heightened partisan rancor of the past few years, this should come as no surprise. In a poll taken in August of 2021, researchers at Marquette University Law School showed that only 60 percent of Americans believed the Supreme Court was doing an adequate job of interpreting the Constitution and coming up with its rulings, down from 66 percent just a year before.[5] It was the sharpest dip in public opinion since they began asking the question in the mid-twentieth century.

During the confirmation hearing of Amy Coney Barrett a few months later, my colleague on the Judiciary Committee, Senator Sheldon Whitehouse said it was "up to us"—the "us" in question being Democrats—"to figure out how to...restore a court that is demonstrably not the organ of big special interests."[6] I found that argument disturbing, in part because it left open the question of just how Democrats intended to "restore" the Court—by adding more justices, perhaps?

Senator Whitehouse called his comments that day "more or less a preview of coming attractions," and regrettably he was right. In the aftermath of Justice Barrett's first session on the Supreme Court, the attacks were relentless.

On December 16, 2021, an op-ed in *The New York Times* declared that the Supreme Court had been "weaponized," its writer comparing the recent opinions to "a drone strike" and writing that the "path of destruction of settled precedent and long-established norms is breathtaking."[7] In previous months, there had been similarly unhinged claims made in public about the Court, many of them linked to the fact that three of its justices had been appointed by President Donald J. Trump, which according to some on the Left, somehow made the Court illegitimate.

Underlying all this negative coverage, though, is the assumption that the Supreme Court is a political body just like Congress and the White House. Some assume that justices who are appointed by Republican presidents are going to behave like Republican elected officials, and that appointees of Democratic presidents will do the same for the other side. But that assumption is wildly inaccurate. In fact, the job of a Supreme Court justice and a United States senator could not be more different. I say that as a United States senator who has spent much of his life following the Supreme Court, has worked at and appeared before the Court, and has even been considered as a potential Supreme Court nominee.

Its chambers are attached neither to the Capitol nor the White House—and with good reason. The Supreme Court's proceedings are supposed to take place literally and figuratively beyond the realm of politics and policy.

So, before embarking on the rest of this book, I think that it's important to remind all Americans what the Supreme Court actually is—and, perhaps more importantly, what it is *not*.

———————

Writing in *The Federalist*, no. 78, Alexander Hamilton correctly referred to the federal judiciary as the "least dangerous" branch of the federal government's three branches.[8] Those words were certainly true at the time, and should always remain true, because the exercise of judicial power is (and should be) uniquely narrow—interpreting laws rather than making them.

As we all learned (or at least *should have* been taught) in grade school, middle school, and high school—but as many in Washington often seem to forget—we have three branches of government in the United States. They're often referred to as being "equal" branches, but that isn't the best way to describe them. They are better referred to as three independent, *coordinate* branches. Each one exists in its own sphere, possessing its own authority that the others do not. One branch must not attempt to exercise the authority of another branch.

Article I of the Constitution creates, restricts, and assigns authority to the Legislative Branch, providing (in Article I, Section 1, Clause 1) that "[a]ll legislative powers [within the federal government] shall be vested in a Congress of the United States, which shall consist of a Senate and a House of Representatives." "Legislative powers" are those required to "legislate," *i.e.*, make laws. Laws are binding rules that are enforced by the government, although law enforcement is an executive function covered under Article II, which we will address separately in a moment. The point is that Congress, being the branch that *makes* federal law, is the branch that decides *what should be*.

By almost any objective standard, that particular authority—the power to decide "what should be," as far as federal law is concerned—makes Congress the most dangerous branch, by a fairly wide margin. The founders understood that danger, and went out of their way to establish several checks on legislators' power. They established term limits for senators and members of the representatives to keep them accountable to the people. They required bills to pass both houses of Congress before becoming law and subjected those bills to presidential veto power (which Congress can only override with a massive two-thirds majority). They denied Congress the power to enforce, administer, or interpret the laws it enacts.

Furthermore, federal law itself was limited to a list of "enumerated" powers that the Constitution itself deems necessarily national in scope. This included declaring war, regulating trade or "commerce" between the states and with foreign nations, coining money, and collecting taxes. Finally, in the Bill of Rights, the Founders specifically laid out things Congress may *not* do (*e.g.*, enact laws restricting free speech, depriving a person of life, liberty, or property without due process of law, or inflicting cruel and unusual punishment), even if such measures would otherwise fall within Congress's already-confined lawmaking authority.

All of the foregoing suggests that those who wrote, signed, and ratified the Constitution had strong opinions about Congress, and went more than out of their way to limit its power. The Constitution—the entire purpose of which is to restrict the exercise of government power—contains more words directed at Congress than anything else, and far more than those directed at either of the other two branches or to the states. Tellingly, it dedicates 2,268 words to the particulars of what Congress may and may not do. Contemporaneous writings and transcripts make clear that the framers were worried about *Congress* exerting an outsized influence on the American people—far more than they worried about any other feature of government.

Some may find this preoccupation curious, given that at the time the Constitution was written, our country was still new, and operating with a Congress that had proven relatively harmless—partly because little time had elapsed since the Revolution, but mostly because Congress had been largely powerless under the Articles of Confederation. In fact, the relative powerlessness of Congress under the Articles of Confederation (along with the corresponding need for a national legislative body capable of achieving a degree of national uniformity among the newly sovereign American states) is precisely what led to the Constitutional Convention of 1787. They came together for the express purpose of expanding the reach of Congress. But they knew that this was dangerous business for one simple reason: the lawmaking power, by its very nature, makes Congress the "most dangerous" of the three branches. So, they spent the most time making sure that we in Congress never accumulated too much power.

In the executive branch, the president of the United States is tasked with implementing and enforcing laws enacted by Congress. In Article II, the Constitution contains about a thousand words laying out the responsibilities of the executive branch, specifying how the president should be elected and when, how the states should choose their electors and the qualifications that a person must have to serve as president.

The legislative and executive branches are political by design. They are made up of elected officials, and the laws they are charged with making (in the case of the legislative branch) and enforcing (in the case of the executive branch) can change according to the will of the people. When the American people want to do something that requires legislation—prohibiting one thing or mandating another—they can do so by petitioning their elected representatives to enact a law. There are, however, some things that the law cannot do. There are certain rights upon which Congress and the executive branch cannot infringe, even if the majority of people in the United States want them to—even if the majority of people are *begging* them to. The founders knew that this might happen, which is why they wrote our Constitution, and soon thereafter, our Bill of Rights. They intended to take our most important freedoms—of speech, the press, and the rest of the ones everyone knows—and enshrine them in a document that was, in effect, safe from future "democratic" mobs that might want to abolish them in later years. The two political branches, both of which are operated by individuals who have sworn an oath to adhere to the Constitution, are expected to refrain from any action prohibited by that document. Constitutional government exists only to the extent that most of those elected to the presidency, the Senate, and the House of Representatives are willing to check their own power, using the Constitution as their guide.

But what happens when they *don't* adhere to constitutional norms of their own volition? In other words, what happens when Congress enacts and the president enforces a law contrary to the restrictions imposed by the Constitution? More to the point, what happens when people of good conscience and sound mind disagree as to the meaning of a particular law or constitutional provision? That's where the *other* branch of the federal government—the Supreme Court "and such inferior courts as Congress may by law establish"—comes into play. It is the job of the judicial branch to resolve such disputes, and resolve "cases or controversies" brought before them. Administered by men and women who, once nominated by the president and confirmed by the Senate, serve "during good behavior"—*i.e.*, for life, as long as they don't do anything to trigger their impeachment and removal—the judicial branch was designed to be essentially immune to popular opinion. Within the judicial branch, insulation from accountability was an essential design feature, not a bug.

In this respect, the judicial branch is fundamentally undemocratic. Sometimes, it's even *anti*-democratic. According to its mandate in Article III of the Constitution, an article that is substantially shorter than both articles that precede it, the judiciary is responsible for resolving specific disputes as to the meaning and application of federal law (whether statutory or constitutional). It has no power to write laws. Nor is it authorized to enforce laws (in fact, it must rely on the Executive Branch to enforce its rulings). Its authority extends only to adjudicating real disputes that arise between real people—not just people who care about the meaning of the law for one reason or another, but people who care *because of the way the law directly affects them in particular.*

Unlike the other branches, the judiciary does not take an affirmative, proactive role in American public life. It doesn't issue "advisory opinions" or otherwise express its views in the abstract, and renders no advice to lawmakers as to the legal, constitutional, or policy implications of any legislative proposal. Nor does it weigh in on bills as they move through the legislative process.

In fact, even *after* a bill becomes a law, the judicial branch still doesn't get involved—not unless or until a dispute arises between two or more parties. Even when such disputes arise, the courts don't undertake an open-ended, comprehensive review of each law at issue (offering opinions as to the precise meaning, scope, and constitutionality of each provision of that law). Instead, they address the issues properly presented to them by the parties, including both (a) questions of law (that is, the plaintiff argues that a particular law means "x," while the defendant insists that it means "y") and (b) questions of fact (*e.g.*, the plaintiff presents evidence showing that the defendant drove through a red light at a particular intersection at 12:31 p.m. on the date in question, while the defendant argues that the plaintiff's evidence on this point isn't credible and is contradicted by other evidence). Questions of law are decided by judges themselves. Questions of fact (insofar as they can't be resolved prior to trial) are decided at trial by the "finder of fact," which is either a judge or a jury (convened by and operating under the direction of a judge), depending on the nature of the case and the preference of the parties. The Constitution protects the right to a jury trial in most civil cases (under the

Seventh Amendment),* and in nearly all criminal cases (under the Sixth Amendment),† although there are exceptions. That said, even where there is a right to a jury trial, the parties may consent to a "bench trial," in which questions of fact are resolved by a judge rather than a jury.

Judicial proceedings come to a presumptive conclusion when the trial court—having resolved all necessary questions of law and fact—issues a final ruling or "judgment." While

---

* The Seventh Amendment provides that, "[i]n Suits at common law, where the value in controversy shall exceed twenty dollars, the right of trial by jury shall be preserved, and no fact tried by a jury, shall be reexamined in any Court of the United States, than according to the rules of the common law." Not every civil action amounts to a suit "at common law." Exceptions include maritime actions, claims against the government, and some actions seeking only equitable remedies.

† The Sixth Amendment provides that, "[i]n all criminal prosecutions, the accused shall enjoy the right to a speedy and public trial, by an impartial jury of the State and district wherein the crime shall have been committed, which district shall have been previously ascertained by law, and to be informed of the nature and cause of the accusation; to be confronted with the witnesses against him; to have compulsory process for obtaining witnesses in his favor, and to have the Assistance of Counsel for his defense." The Supreme Court has ruled that criminal prosecutions against juvenile defendants don't qualify as "criminal prosecutions" for purposes relevant to the Sixth Amendment right to a jury trial. *See McKeiver* v. *Pennsylvania*, 403 U.S. 528 (1971).

many cases are resolved in a way that produces a clear "winner" and a clear "loser," it's not uncommon for each party to secure a partial win and a partial loss.

Losing parties nearly always have the right to challenge or "appeal" a judgment entered by the trial court. Courts of appeals (which in the federal judicial system are called "circuit courts," while trial courts are referred to as "district courts") don't hear testimony from witnesses or receive evidence because they aren't finders of fact; their task is a narrow one, focusing on whether to "affirm" or "reverse" any part of the lower court's judgment—*i.e.*, whether to let it stand or over-turn it. The appellate court will nearly always defer to fac-tual findings made by the judge or jury at trial. When they don't, it's usually because the evidence underlying a particu-lar finding was either improperly admitted in the earlier trial, or because that evidence cannot fairly be read to support the finding at issue.

Each appeal will typically come to an end with an order either affirming or reversing the judgment rendered by the trial court, although in some cases the appellate court will remand the case back to the trial court for further proceedings, and in some cases even a new trial. That is normally where the Supreme Court comes into the picture—maybe.

I say "maybe" because the Supreme Court, unlike circuit courts and most of their state-court appellate counterparts, has considerable discretion over its docket. In a typical year, there may be as many as 10,000 (more commonly 8,000) cases brought to the Supreme Court, with at least one party seeking to reverse or otherwise modify a lower-court judgment. In nearly all of those cases, the Court leaves the lower-court ruling intact simply by issuing a one-line order denying discretionary review, which is known as "certiorari." By denying certiorari, the Supreme Court leaves the lower-court ruling intact without setting new precedent, or even sending any signal as to whether the lower court acted properly.

The Supreme Court makes clear that, with only rare exceptions, it is "not a court of error correction," meaning that its objective is normally *not* to review all lower-court rulings to ensure correctness (doing so would be physically impossible, given the sheer volume of cases), but rather to focus its efforts on deciding cases with an eye toward resolving disagreements or "splits" among the lower courts—that is, to grant certiorari when two or more lower courts have adopted inconsistent interpretations of the same important provision of federal law. Using these "circuit splits" as its typical guidepost, the Court grants certiorari in only about 80 cases per term, which amounts to an average of roughly 1 percent of all cases brought to its attention each year. Far from a random sampling of all cases that move through the judicial system each year, these cases tend to involve unusually difficult legal questions.

Ultimately, however, what cases the Court agrees to decide is itself a matter of discretion. As long as at least four justices agree that a case is worthy of granting certiorari, the Court will decide the case. And in the absence of four justices voting to grant certiorari, the Court will (absent very rare circumstances in which the Court is legally required to act, and doesn't have the option of simply denying certiorari) leave the case alone completely—regardless of how interesting, important, controversial, or even wrong the lower-court ruling might have been.

If your only perception of how the Supreme Court worked was formed by elements of the mainstream media and the entertainment industry, it might look something like this: You might imagine its public proceedings and internal deliberations to be full of partisan bickering and intense controversy. You might imagine the justices fighting with each other late into the night, leaning over the conference table to hurl insults (or at least politically and emotionally charged comments) at one another—with those justices appointed by Republican presidents on one side of the table (and each controversy), and those appointed by Democrats on the other. Mercifully, those impressions of the Court, while held by many, are wildly inaccurate.

In fact, even though the Supreme Court tends not to decide easy cases, and normally focuses its efforts on unusually difficult questions of federal law—as to which lower courts (despite their impressive training, expertise, and best efforts) have been unable to agree—most of the justices agree with each other most of the time, regardless of which president appointed them.

Even though the cases the Supreme Court decides are unusually difficult (otherwise, they would likely escape the

Court's notice), most of them are *not* decided by the slimmest of margins. In fact, the most common configuration cases the Court decides in any given year are decided either unanimously or nearly so. The process is deliberative, painstaking, methodical, and largely devoid of emotion: Each justice reviews the arguments—first in writing, then in an intense, hour-long conversation of sorts, known as "oral argument." Within a day or two following oral argument, the nine justices gather in a conference room. The justices address each case separately, in the same order in which it was argued. The chief justice speaks first, typically summarizing his or her views on the case at hand in no more than a few sentences (*e.g.*, "The lower court read the statute to mean 'x,' but I read it to mean 'y,' so I think we should reverse"). The associate justices then speak in order of seniority, each summarizing his or her views with as few words as possible (*e.g.*, "I agree with the Chief, and think we should reverse," or "I think the lower court's reading of the statute was correct, so I think we should affirm"). The entire process tends to consume no more than a few minutes and—while observed exclusively by the nine members of the Court (not even a single law clerk or secretary is allowed in the room while this is happening)—would almost never qualify as the kind of content fit for a must-see television experience. Within the Supreme Court's unique microculture, it is simply understood that these "conference" deliberations are not opportunities for grandstanding, airing personal grievances, or otherwise expressing emotion. If there were such a thing as an emotional Richter scale—one that could somehow allow us to measure the collective emotions produced by a meeting in the same way we measure the intensity of earthquakes—these members-only conferences very rarely "move the needle" at all.

Many Americans (including many lawyers) are surprised and even a little disappointed when they learn that lengthy knock-down, drag-out fights among members of the Supreme Court are practically nonexistent, perhaps because they have bought into the narrative that the Court functions like a political body. But it doesn't. And if you think about it, we shouldn't wish it were otherwise. If we believe that the job of the judiciary is to resolve disputes regarding the law's meaning (and we do), we should want the Court to be driven by a sincere desire to find the right answer—an endeavor that shouldn't be full of emotion.

The Supreme Court appears to agree. For nearly all of its history, the Court has decided cases unanimously far more often than through closely divided decisions. Even in 2016, a year in which the Court decided an unusually large number of politically charged cases, more than half of the cases argued were ultimately decided by unanimous votes.[9] In those cases, there were no dissents. Everyone agreed.

Even in the term concluding in June 2021 (in which the Court was again called upon to resolve an unusually large number of contentious issues)—and after the confirmation of Associate Justice Amy Coney Barrett (whose confirmation, many insisted, would hasten the Court's decline into an ugly, partisan institution, dominated by six justices appointed by Republican presidents)—the rate of unanimous decisions actually went *up*. By the middle of 2021, during Justice Barrett's first year on the bench, an ABC News report found that the Court had handed down more unanimous opinions than it had in the past seven years.[10]

But like close games in sports, split decisions rendered by the Supreme Court (particularly those involving a vote of five to four) often receive the most public attention, so you're more likely to hear about them on the news. They are the cases that tend to inspire public protests, op-eds, and, more recently, calls to change the composition of the Supreme Court so that it better reflects the so-called "will of the people."

But even in that context, we should not exaggerate the role that the Supreme Court plays. Even in hot-button cases involving disputed questions of law and public policy, when the Supreme Court issues a ruling, that ruling finally resolves only the dispute between the parties before the Court in that particular case. Notwithstanding the precedent that ruling may establish, there are myriad ways in which that precedent won't foreclose future public debate and discussion of the underlying issue.

It is hardly unusual for Congress to change laws in response to a Supreme Court ruling. For example, in *Ledbetter* v. *Goodyear Tire and Rubber Co.*, the Supreme Court in 2007 interpreted provisions of Title VII of the Civil Rights Act of 1964 addressing the period of time in which a plaintiff must file suit challenging employment discrimination. After that ruling left the plaintiff in that case, Lilly Ledbetter, without a cause of action against her employer, Congress amended Title VII to make the law more permissive than it had been, as interpreted by the Court. Thus, far from foreclosing future debate, discussion, and legislation regarding the issue, the Supreme Court's ruling—while controversial and resulting from a five-to-four vote—*prompted* legislation by drawing attention to the issue. Had the Court not interpreted the statute as it did, opting for the more comfortable and politically palatable interpretation of legislation Congress had enacted rather than the *correct* one, it would have shielded Congress from accountability and encouraged Congress to act with less precision in the future.

The type of outcome we saw in *Ledbetter* (in which a Supreme Court ruling interpreting statutory text prompted a legislative fix by Congress) is, of course, not always possible. Where, for example, a Supreme Court ruling involves not the interpretation of statutory text (which can be changed by an act of Congress) but a provision of the Constitution (which itself can be changed only by a constitutional amendment), a simple legislative fix won't be an option.

Nevertheless, a Supreme Court ruling on a constitutional issue—even one invalidating a particular government action as unconstitutional—doesn't always mean that the underlying issue is untouchable or that the American people are powerless to it through their elected representatives. Sometimes it just means that the wrong government (state or federal) acted.

Sometimes it means that the wrong *branch* of government (legislative, executive, or judicial) acted. Other times it might mean that those responsible for the constitutional violation may still accomplish what they were trying to do, but need to do so under a slightly different theory or using different language.

The future implications—and thus the controversy—attached to Supreme Court rulings are perhaps most prominently on display when the Court concludes that a certain government violates a particular provision of the Constitution. This is especially true when the ruling in question leaves little room for argument about whether another government or branch thereof may act, or whether in the future a slightly different, but constitutionally valid path might be available to the government actors deemed to have acted unconstitutionally. Such rulings are controversial specifically because they tend to be *counter*-democratic—that is, they invalidate government policies, in spite of how popular they might be with voters, and take otherwise-debatable matters effectively beyond debate within our system of government. That kind of outcome understandably tends to leave many voters feeling both angry and frustrated.

That has certainly happened in the wake of *Roe* v. *Wade*, in which the Supreme Court held that the Constitution prohibits many government-imposed restrictions on abortion. Americans who view unborn human life as worth protecting view *Roe* and its progeny as an unwarranted impediment not only to their preferred policy outcome, but as incompatible with representative government and its fundamental responsibility to protect life, liberty, and property. Wrong as I believe it was, *Roe* purported to be grounded in the Constitution, and is consequently not the kind of ruling that can be remedied easily through legislative action. It takes debatable—and indeed, passionately debated—matters beyond debate, and does so without justification under the Constitution. That's what makes rulings like *Roe* so dangerous to our form of government.

That, however, is not to say that all rulings invalidating government acts as unconstitutional are bad or that they should be avoided wherever possible. Such rulings need not be rare or issued with timidity; they just need to be *correct*. Indeed, they are part of the deal. Arguably, the most important function of the American Constitution is to constrain government power—even where (indeed, especially where) popular opinion might prescribe a different outcome. Warrantless searches and seizures by police, government restrictions on free speech and the free exercise of religion, and uncompensated takings of private property by government are just a few examples of the kinds of things that—even where popular, as they might be in some circumstances—we have properly taken beyond reasonable debate under the Constitution. In this sense, the Constitution acts as a counter-majoritarian control on government. The Supreme Court, as the top adjudicative body within the federal government, plays an essential role in ensuring that these otherwise-debatable matters remain largely beyond debate unless or until the Constitution is amended to provide otherwise. None of us—or at least none of us who understand that government power is inherently dangerous unless appropriately constrained—would want to strip the Court of its power to interpret the Constitution, and thus identify certain actions as out of bounds. Thus, it's wrong to suggest that the Court should avoid invalidating government actions as unconstitutional.

Just the same, the Court's power must be used responsibly and within the bounds established by the Constitution. To whatever degree it invalidates as unconstitutional a government action that comports with the Constitution, it strips the American people of their right to adopt, through their elected representatives, government policies consistent with their own preferences. On the other hand, when the Court issues a ruling declining to invalidate a government act amounting to a clear violation of the Constitution, it deprives Americans of their constitutional rights, leaving them at the whim of government actors. Thus, we shouldn't want a Court that is either categorically eager or instinctively reluctant to invalidate government action. We should just want a Court that will properly read, interpret, and apply the Constitution—based on what it says, rather than what individual justices might *wish* it said. And while not everyone will agree as to what each provision of the Constitution says, correctly interpreting it should always be the objective.

People will not always agree as to what the correct interpretation of the Constitution is in every case, and there will always be people who disagree with the majority opinion of Supreme Court decisions. But this is simply how our constitutional system is designed to work. To call for the Supreme Court to be reformed for political reasons is to fundamentally misunderstand what the Court is and what it should do. It is a place where politics, at least in theory, do not matter, and where the noise of public opinion has no place. All that matters in the courtroom, especially in the hallowed chamber of the Supreme Court, is whether a given law does or does not violate the words of the Constitution. The words of that document, contrary to what some liberal theorists would have you believe, have meaning. When they were put in a certain order, written down, and codified as law in 1789, they became the foundation upon which our judicial system was built.

"The Constitution is not a living document," as it was put by the great justice Antonin Scalia during a speech at Southern Methodist University in 2013. "It is dead, dead, dead."[11]

By this, Justice Scalia meant, quite simply, that laws mean precisely what they meant to the people who adopted them. Good lawyers, and good justices, would do well to take his advice, especially when it comes to cases that come before the highest court in the land.

During his time as solicitor general, my father won a very high percentage of the cases that he argued before the Court. This included 27 out of 29 cases that he overturned from the

Ninth Circuit, one of the more erratic and volatile federal courts in the country at the time. In large part, he was able to win so many of those cases because he was a "lawyer's lawyer." He knew that as a lawyer, his first—and, really, his *only*—job was to give his client the best defense that he could.

But my dad knew that the Supreme Court was no place for politics. He only wanted to adhere to the Constitution. Sometimes, that put him at odds with the administration, and with the public perception of his job. As he neared the end of his tenure, he stated in an interview: "There has been a notion that my job is to press the administration's policies at every turn and announce true conservative principles through the pages of my briefs. It is not. I'm the solicitor general, not the pamphleteer general."[12]

The point being, I suppose, that a serious lawyer with a case before the Supreme Court should not be trying to argue political points. If representing the government itself (as the solicitor general does) they are not representing the merits of a particular policy according to the will of the people or even the will of a president. Far more often, they are arguing that the particular government action does or does not align with the law and the Constitution, a document that has fostered the development of the greatest human flourishing in the history of civilization.

The Constitution is a wonderful document not only because it is ours, or because it was written by wise men raised up by God for that very purpose, but because it *works*. When our judges and elected officials constrain their behavior as directed by the words of the Constitution, considering what they meant to the people who enacted them at the moment they were enacted, our republic functions as it should. It has been this way for hundreds of years, and if we continue to act according to the principles set forth in our founding documents, it will continue to be this way for hundreds more.

CHAPTER TWO

How We Got to Nine

CONTRARY TO WHAT YOU MIGHT THINK, ESPECIALLY given the title and overall mission of this book, there's nothing special about the number nine. This number doesn't come from the Bible, the common law, or any of our founding documents. Rather, the number nine was arrived at by way of a few ordinary political decisions over about two centuries—what might be called a long series of historical accidents, one occurring as a result of the last, until they finally brought us, somehow, to the right place.

Which, if you think about it, is not a bad definition of American history in general.

The United States Constitution says nothing about the number of justices who should serve on the Supreme Court. As we have already seen, it says very little about the courts at all. For this reason, the Court had to spend the majority of its early existence deciding for itself what role it would play in the government of the United States. This wasn't always easy, and it wasn't always clear what the right path was. But luckily, there were a few early luminaries who stepped up, made the right decisions, and made the Supreme Court what it is today.

It is not an exaggeration to say that without these key leaders, the United States might not exist at all, certainly not in the form that we know it.

The first among them is John Marshall, a chief justice who is often cited as the founder of many important principles that the Court still follows today. He is so influential, in fact, that the years before he became chief justice in 1801 are often spoken of as a kind of "lost decade" for the Court, a period in which it groped around in the dark and attempted with little success to figure out what it was. Writing in *The American Supreme Court*, his landmark study of the Court and its role in American life, the historian Robert McCloskey writes of this period as having "the quality of a play's opening moments with minor characters exchanging trivialities while they and the audience await the appearance of the star."[1]

Looking back, it is relatively clear that McCloskey, and other historians who have made similar claims, are correct. Back in the late 1790s, the Court had very little idea what its main role was. That said, it was generally understood that the Supreme Court—and the judiciary in general—would be an immensely important part of American life. Writing to John Jay in October 1789, just a few weeks after being named the first president of the United States, George Washington wrote that the judiciary was "that department which must be considered as the keystone of our political fabric."[2]

Whether Washington believed this or not, he certainly appears to have acted like it. "In no area," writes Ron Chernow in his biography of Washington, "did [he] exert more painstaking effort than in selected judges."[3] This began with his selection of John Jay, a respected lawyer and the coauthor, with Alexander Hamilton and James Madison, of *The Federalist Papers*, as the nation's first chief justice. At the time, Jay was thrilled at the prospect. For years, he had dedicated himself to the law with every fiber of his being, fighting for property rights and freedom from taxation for the colonies. He was an ardent defender of the new Constitution and a dedicated student of the principles it stood for. He believed, and not without reason, that a seat on the highest court in the land would be a wonderful capstone to a long career in the law.

This, sadly, proved not to be the case. In the ten years that John Jay would serve as chief justice, the Court did very little, and it was largely forgotten by the American public. During this time, the Court heard only a few dozen cases, and its decisions in those cases did not make much of an impact on life in the United States.

Most of the trouble was procedural. For one thing, the Court did not yet know how to craft its opinions so that they would make an impact. In those days, when it was time to hand down their decisions, each justice—all six of them, one for each federal judicial district—would write his own opinion, restating the facts of the case and interpreting them in his own unique way. From contemporary records, it is clear that very few people read these opinions, with the possible exception of the parties, the lawyers involved, and the justices themselves.

The practice, known as writing *seriatim*, made it nearly impossible to figure out what the Court was actually trying to say at any given time. The justices were speaking with five different voices rather than one unified voice.

But the confusion was hardly the worst part of the job. The travel was. About twice a year, each justice would be required to leave his home and "ride circuit," commuting by horseback to sit on the bench of whichever of these six original circuit courts to which he'd been assigned. This was a cumbersome task, and it meant that justices often spent very little time reading and writing about the law—which, if you hadn't guessed, is a big part of being a judge. It also made for delays. On February 1, 1790, for instance, the first time that the Court ever met, the meeting had to be postponed for a day because three of the justices were stuck on the dirt roads into New York City.[4]

For the first few years of the Court's existence, in fact, its justices met primarily on the cramped first floor of City Hall in Philadelphia, sharing space with the local mayor's judiciary.[5] When that room wasn't available, they resorted to meeting in private homes. Conditions on the circuit courts, where the justices were forced to travel several times a year, were much worse. Due to the lack of federal courthouses, most early trials took place in roadside taverns or rented-out office buildings. The Supreme Court would not have a true home for decades— or centuries, if you consider that the massive building of white marble we know today was not completed until 1935, nearly 150 years after the Court was created by the Constitution.

If you think that all this sounds...well, let's say, "not desirable," you'd be exactly right.

In 1801, John Jay, who had taken a great deal of time off during his tenure as chief justice to travel abroad and negotiate trade agreements with England, was offered the opportunity to resume his duties by President John Adams, who had just succeeded George Washington to become the nation's second president. Given that justices were unique among federal officials in that their terms of office didn't expire, it was generally expected that they would serve for life. The job, although not glamorous, was still the most prestigious in the legal profession. But when Jay was given the official offer by President Adams, he turned it down. He had seen too much of the Supreme Court, and evidently, he had been dismayed by what he had seen.

"I left the Bench," he wrote in a letter to Adams, "perfectly convinced that under a System so defective, it would not obtain the Energy weight and Dignity which are essential to its affording due support to the national Government; nor acquire the public Confidence and Respect, which, as the last Resort of the Justice of the Nation, it should possess."[6]

Looking back, this seems harsh, if not terribly shortsighted. (Although many of today's jurists might say the same thing if the job required them to saddle up and ride from Philadelphia to Massachusetts twice a year to resolve mundane disputes involving obscure federal statutes and stolen chickens.) But Jay was not alone. During the first few years of the Court's existence, it was not always a sure thing that those asked to sit on the highest bench in the land would agree to do so. Edmund Pendleton, a lawyer from Virginia who had played a major role in shaping the Constitution, said "no." So did Oliver Ellsworth, who had fought hard to ratify the Constitution in his native South Carolina. This arguably suggests that there was a lack of clarity regarding what the Court was, and even less on what it should be doing.

In *The Federalist Papers*, Alexander Hamilton and John Jay had put forth a few ideas about how the Court should use the power granted it by Article III of the Constitution. So had the men who wrote the Constitution itself. But no one could quite reach an agreement. Some believed that it should be a political body just like Congress and the executive branch, playing a vital and explicit role in the crafting of legislation. Others thought that it shouldn't play much of a role at all.

According to Alexander Hamilton and other Federalists like him, one of the primary functions of the Court would be to resolve disputes regarding the meaning of the law. After applying the law and precedent to the facts of the case, the Court could also decide whether the law at issue aligned with the Constitution. The Court, in other words, would be the final arbiter of whether a given law was constitutional. Today, that might seem obvious. We have been living with a Supreme Court that has performed this exact function for years. But it was far from obvious at the time.

It was also a drastic step to take, given that the balance of power between the branches was so precarious at the time. As a result, the Court did not declare any laws unconstitutional for the first thirty years of its existence. In general, if you look back at these years, it seems that the Court was attempting to achieve a balance that was not always easy to strike. There were several opportunities for the Court, whose members spent a whole lot of time sitting around and making grand pronouncements about what the Court should be doing, to take an active role in politics. This, as we know with the benefit of hindsight, would have been the Court's undoing, ruining the one thing that separates it from all the other branches.

In 1793, for instance, President George Washington came to the Court with a few questions about the Neutrality Proclamation, which would define the position of the United States on conducting foreign wars. Washington wanted to know whether some of the actions he was taking would run afoul of existing laws. But the Court refused, insisting that issuing "advisory opinions"—that is, opinions that don't involve one party bringing a suit against another, and instead only "advise" one party on how to behave—was not among the jobs given to the judiciary by the Constitution.[7] They refused other cases on similar grounds. Much like the authors of the Constitution, the early justices knew that every action they took would set precedent. This was especially important in the law, which relies heavily on past decisions; that is, one case builds on the ones that have come before it, hopefully leading to a cohesive, coherent, and comprehensible body of law.

In some ways, the task might have been even harder for the

justices than it had been for the framers of the Constitution. They were not often in the same room, and when they were, it was usually to work out the drab business of statutory interpretation and other tasks essential to the resolution of both large and own small disputes. Long before it was fashionable, they worked out of their own houses, conducting the majority of their work in living rooms and home offices. (In this sense, and in many others, they were before their time.) Still, in reading their history, it becomes clear that they knew every action they took had to be solid, and solid in the most literal sense of the word—which, from the Latin *solidus*, means "firm, whole, undivided, entire."

The early Court was all about balance, and one wrong move could upset that balance with devastating results for the country.

What it needed was a fair, clear-minded jurist who would be able not only to hear cases and rule fairly on them, but also consider the implications of every step that he took and word that he wrote, remaining ever mindful that his words would have drastic effects for decades to come.

Luckily, that's exactly what the Court got.

———

When John Marshall was appointed to the Supreme Court, he was forty-six years old. He had grown up in colonial Virginia and fought alongside many of our other founders in the Revolutionary War. Described by one biographer as "a tall, genial man with penetrating eyes and a shock of unruly hair," he hated Thomas Jefferson and revered Alexander Hamilton, whom he considered one of the nation's most essential founders.[8] His opinion on the politics of the two men, naturally, ran along similar lines. For just a few months, he was the secretary of state under President John Adams. But when Adams's first choice for the chief justiceship, John Jay, dropped out of the running unexpectedly, he was promoted—or demoted, depending on your view of the matter—to chief justice of the Supreme Court, but not before suggesting rather stridently that Adams go with someone else.

"I believe," Adams is rumored to have said to Marshall, "that I must nominate you."[9]

Little did he know that he, along with the five other justices on the Court at the time, was about to shape the institution that he would serve for the next three decades.

The most famous case of Marshall's life, the one that is still often taught on the first day of every constitutional law course in the United States, began when Thomas Jefferson defeated John Adams in the election of 1800. By that time, President Adams had become immensely unpopular, even among ardent Federalists like Alexander Hamilton and John Jay who had once supported him. Throughout his presidency, Adams had spoken out in favor of censoring freedom of speech, led our nation toward war with France, and spent much of his term traveling to other states and on long vacations with his wife, Abigail.

Jefferson, on the other hand, still enjoyed a stellar reputation among early Americans. He had been a vital member of George Washington's cabinet, and was known as a kind of thought leader at the time. But he had a dark side, too, as anyone who has ever read into his private affairs knows. His campaign against John Adams had been one of the most vicious in American history—which, admittedly, was only about a decade old at the time—but it would hold the record for years. In a pamphlet, Jefferson's supporters cast Adams as having "a hideous hermaphroditical character which has neither the force and firmness of a man, not the gentleness and sensibility of a woman." Even in our times, that seems harsh. Then, when the election finally came, the winner wasn't decided for many weeks.

The hatred between the two men was palpable. As a result, the defeat made President Adams despondent. In those days, due to a long since replaced provision of the Constitution that is hard to imagine today, the person who came second in a presidential race served as the vice president. This approach would be abolished a few years later, but that wasn't what mattered to Adams. In a race that had, in some sense, defined our modern two-party republic, Adams's Federalist Party was going to lose the judiciary. So Adams came up with a plot to appoint as many judges and justices as he could before his term expired, thus denying Jefferson the opportunity to do so. It was, in so many words, a last-ditch effort to stuff the government full of Adams's preferred political appointees. Over the course of his final days in office, Adams drafted a bill that created sixteen circuit court positions, several more justices of the peace, and reduced the size of the Supreme Court from six members to five. It was the first instance of nakedly political Court packing in our nation's history. It was a bad idea then, and it's a bad idea now.

In the first days of the new Jefferson administration, most of Adams's new judges took the bench. They served in high and low courts all over the country. The man who had signed these commissions, in fact, was John Marshall, who served as President Adams's final secretary of state. But there was an error. In a rush to get the nominations out, the administration had failed to properly deliver the commission of a man named William Marbury. Marbury was a leader of the Federalist Party in Maryland who had proven himself to be loyal. His promotion to a federal judgeship would have meant, among other things, a pay raise. But although the commission had been signed and sealed, it wasn't delivered due to a clerical error.

Believing he was entitled to the judgeship, Marbury appeared before the Supreme Court, seeking a writ that would force James Madison, Thomas Jefferson's new secretary of state, to hand over the commission and make him a judge.

At the time, John Marshall and the justices had a choice to make. Either they could rule in Marbury's favor and demand that James Madison hand over the commission, giving the new administration an order that they would surely ignore, or they could side with Jefferson's administration, sending an implicit message that they were against Adams's political agenda. If they took the first course of action, they would look weak and ineffectual, and if they took the second course, they would seem like just another political branch, siding with the party in power and going along with every whim of the executive branch.

Instead, Marshall chose a middle road, one that would have a profound effect on the American Supreme Court as we know it today. In his majority opinion, Marshall admitted that the Jefferson administration *should* have handed over the commission for Marbury's judgeship, but concluded that the Supreme Court was not the appropriate tribunal to grant the relief sought by Marbury. The Court, he wrote, does not have the power to issue writs of the kind that Marbury was looking for. He pointed out that, although the judiciary act Adams signed seemed to give that power to the Court, that act violated the Constitution, and was therefore invalid. This opinion, once and for all, established the principle—which seems so obvious in hindsight—that the Supreme Court of the United States has the power to declare a law unconstitutional. It is the decision that made the Court what it is today.

From there, Marshall continued to help define the Court as we know it. During the early 1800s, for instance, he did away with the practice of having each justice write his own opinion in each case. This practice, he knew, had prevented the Court from speaking as the Court, and it would be much better to have one, clear voice. Of course, the voice he preferred to hear was usually his own. During those first years, it was Marshall himself who wrote most of the opinions, on everything from imports and war to the relatively less important business of taxes and federal statutes.[10]

Today, there is a large statue of John Marshall prominently displayed inside the Supreme Court. If you enter the building on the ground floor, you have to walk past him—just as anyone hoping to enter the legal profession must first confront Marshall's ideas about the law, and the decades of precedents that he set.

When John Marshall died in 1835, he left behind a Supreme Court that had operated under his direction for decades. He had been the chief justice for more than thirty years by that point, handing down rulings in the Court's dark, cramped quarters while four presidents came and went. He had seen Jeffersonian Democracy become ascendant and the Federalist recede slowly into the background.

During the years that he was on the Court, Justice Marshall had done more than perhaps anyone else in our nation's history ever would to determine what role, precisely, the Supreme Court should play in the United States government. He, along with his associate justices, helped to establish the principles of judicial review—the ability of the Court to declare a state or federal law unconstitutional, without which the Court might play a more minor role today—and he was able to carefully avoid questions that had nothing to do with the Court's mission, establishing once and for all that the Court should be a fundamentally apolitical institution. The Court's role should, in the words of Marshall's friend Alexander Hamilton, be "not active but deliberative."[11]

Now, I happen to believe that if modern experience has shown us anything, it's that a passive judge can do just as much damage as an activist. Our era is filled with examples of such rulings. But on principle, Hamilton seems to have been correct. The judiciary does not reach out. It does not issue advisory opinions. It does not assume a political posture in any case. It neither acts nor refuses to act based on any outside consideration—not even its own image—no matter how weighty the controversy at hand. These were all principles established by John Marshall, and his successors do well by following them.

Of course, the nation was still young. Precedents tend to gather more strength over time. In the United States at the time of John Marshall and Thomas Jefferson, there was not a whole lot of precedent to rely on, and what existed was still quite recent. In fact, when the federal government moved its headquarters from Philadelphia to its new capital in Washington, DC, in the early nineteenth century, the entirety of its official records—judicial opinions, correspondence, and the minutes taken during cabinet meetings—fit into just eight regular-sized boxes.[12] Even after a few seemingly momentous years in world history, there was more work to be done than ever in shaping the nation and its courts.

Sadly, the years to come were also filled with spectacular failures of the judicial branch. The 1800s produced some of the darkest episodes in the history of the Supreme Court—occasions when it failed to rule correctly, overstepped its constitutional mandate, or acted according to the personal beliefs of the justices rather than the clear facts of a given case.

Looking back, it is something of a miracle that the nation survived.

One of these decisions, as every elementary school student learns, concerned the case of a man named Dred Scott. Over fifty years old at the time his case went before the Court, Scott had been born a slave in Virginia in 1799, and then moved to Missouri. During his life, his owners took him from Missouri, where slavery was legal, into Illinois and Wisconsin (which was not yet a state), where it wasn't. Scott sued in a series of federal courts to claim that when he entered free territory, he was automatically free, even after he was taken back to a slave state.

When the case reached the Supreme Court, Chief Justice Roger Taney ruled that Black people are not "included, and were not intended to be included, under the word 'citizens' in the Constitution, and can therefore claim none of the rights and privileges which that instrument provides and secures for citizens of the United States."[13]

That opinion, has rightly lived in infamy since the day it was handed down. Most people knew it was wrong at the time, and they know it today. The tension between those who believed that the Court should have heard Scott's case and those who didn't was so intense, in fact, that it led to the Civil War.

It also began one of the great Court-packing fights in our history.

At the beginning of the war (and of Abraham Lincoln's presidency), the Supreme Court was known, in the words of the *Pioneer News* in St. Paul, as "the last stronghold of Southern power."

"The Supreme Court has been," the newspaper concluded on January 3, 1862, "the agent of the southern statesmen; its sympathies have been altogether with the south; in construing our laws it has never omitted an opportunity of showing its regard for the institution of slavery...it has been either silent and sullen or actively engaged in throwing obstacles in the way of the administration."[14]

As states began seceding from the union in larger and larger numbers, so too did Justice John Archibald Campbell, who, as a native of Georgia, had more sympathy with the Confederacy than with the Union. During his first year in office, President Lincoln said in a speech that the country had "generally...outgrown our present judicial system," moving just a few months later to introduce the Judiciary Act of 1862, which would completely reorganize the federal circuit court system. He also appointed three Republican justices, evening the balance of power somewhat.

But as the war went on, it became clear that he and

the Republicans had not gone far enough in reshaping the Supreme Court to their current needs. As a consequence, they added one seat to the Court, bringing the number up to ten— the highest it has ever been—and finally delivered to Lincoln a group of justices that would rule the way he wanted them to.

In hindsight, you might say that this was a net positive. The cause of the Union during the Civil War was just, after all, and the country needed a decisive victory against the Confederacy. If the Supreme Court wasn't giving Lincoln what he wanted, didn't he have every right, in the name of justice, to change the Court until they did? Maybe. But it's important to note that political moves like this one, especially in times of great polarization, only lead to similar moves in the future—and, as with most fights, those moves tend to get more drastic with time.

In 1865, after President Lincoln was shot and Andrew Johnson took over, the new president tried to appoint loyal secessionists to the Supreme Court in retaliation for what Lincoln had done during the war. If it hadn't been for Congress, which was still full of Republicans willing to deny him these appointments at all costs, he might have succeeded. The most prominent result of his efforts, fortunately, was the Judicial Circuits Act of 1866, which took away three seats from the Court, bringing the number down to seven in order to ensure that Johnson wouldn't be able to appoint any justices. These seats, however, were not eliminated right away. The idea was to eliminate the seats in the only manner allowed under the Constitution, which involves allowing each justice to remain on the bench until death, retirement, or removal from office. Only two vacancies arose during Johnson's presidency, with the deaths of justices John Catron (in 1865) and James Moore Wayne (in 1867), leaving the Court with eight justices.

Then, with the passage of the Judiciary Act of 1869, in order to prevent tie votes and to establish one justice for each of the country's nine circuits, Congress added one more seat for Joseph P. Bradley. Two years later, Congress would abolish the need for justices to "ride circuit" as well, allowing them to stay in Washington, DC, and hear cases.

Finally, after a long series of political fights, we had arrived at nine.

CHAPTER THREE

The First Progressive Fights

B Y THE BEGINNING OF THE TWENTIETH CENTURY, IT seemed that the Supreme Court of the United States was finally beginning to find its rhythm. In the more than three decades since the passage of the Judiciary Act of 1869, there had been no serious talk of adding more seats to the Court. The number of justices, which had remained in flux throughout the middle of the nineteenth century—along with just about everything else in the United States—seemed to be stuck at nine for good.

During the first years of that century, those nine justices conducted themselves in the manner prescribed by the Constitution. They heard cases, studied the facts, and did their best to apply the words of the Constitution fairly in every case. But there were also factions emerging within the Court's chambers, and the rifts between those factions were growing. Before long, those rifts would grow considerably, creating instability within the federal judicial system.

One of these rifts grew out of a particular interpretation of the Fourteenth Amendment that had become popular in the late 1890s. At the time this amendment was ratified in 1868, essentially for the purpose of stamping out badges of slavery and prohibiting states from treating people differently on the basis of race, the wording had seemed relatively straightforward. The first and most salient section of it reads as follows:

> All persons born or naturalized in the United States, and subject to the jurisdiction thereof, are citizens of the United States and of the state wherein they reside. No state shall make or enforce any law which shall abridge the privileges or immunities of citizens of the United States; nor shall any state deprive any person of life, liberty, or property, without due process of law; nor deny to any person within its jurisdiction the equal protection of the laws.

On its face, this language shouldn't have confused anyone. In fact, many of these words were not even new. Some of them had been carried over from the Fifth Amendment, which prevented the *federal* government from depriving people of "life, liberty, or property without due process of law." This new amendment extended those same prohibitions to state governments; while the Thirteenth Amendment ended the practice of slavery and the Fifteenth Amendment extended the right to vote to former slaves and people of all races, the Fourteenth Amendment imposed additional restrictions on states to make sure that they would never again deprive American citizens of due process or equal protection (*i.e.*, the right to be treated equally and fairly under the law without regard to immutable characteristics like race).

But a few decades after the Fourteenth Amendment was ratified, a handful of enterprising lawyers representing wealthy individuals and corporations—including those who owned railroads, factories, and other businesses enjoying an unusually robust, postwar boom—began appearing before federal judges to argue that the Fourteenth Amendment should shield them from certain state laws that increased the cost of doing business. Some laws, in their view, were unconstitutional because they trampled on their right to enter into contracts and otherwise manage their business affairs as they deemed fit.

When these cases started to reach the Supreme Court, the Court's rulings started to fracture along political and ideological lines to a relatively unprecedented degree. That, in turn, pushed the Court into the public spotlight, and not in a good way.

Perhaps the most famous among these cases was *Lochner* v. *New York*. Decided in 1905, this case helped set the tone for the period of generally consistent jurisprudence that became known as the "Lochner Era." In *Lochner*, the Supreme Court invalidated a New York state law limiting the hours of bakery workers (to no more than ten hours per day or 60 hours per week). In a controversial, five-to-four decision, the Court concluded that both workers and employers have a constitutionally protected right to negotiate the terms of employment contracts without state interference. As the Court explained, "[t]he right to purchase or to sell labor is part of the liberty protected by" the Fourteenth Amendment's Due Process Clause "unless there are circumstances which exclude the right." The majority opinion, authored by Associate Justice Rufus Peckham, reasoned that:

> Statutes of the nature of that under review, limiting the hours in which grown and intelligent men may labor to earn their living, are mere meddlesome interferences with the rights of the individual, and they are not saved from condemnation by the claim that they are passed in the exercise of the police power and upon the subject of the health of the individual whose rights are interfered with, unless there by some fair ground, reasonable in and of itself, to say that there is material danger to the public health, or to the health of the employees, if the hours of labor are not curtailed. If this be not clearly the case, the individuals whose rights are thus made the subject of legislative interference are under the protection of the Federal Constitution regarding their liberty of contract as well as of person; and the legislature of the state has no power to limit their right as proposed in this statute.

In other words, having found that it simply is not "reasonable" for a state to conclude that the health and safety of its people will be advanced by maximum-hour laws, the Court deemed such laws not only unnecessary and unwise, but unconstitutional.

It's worth remembering that in taking this aggressive action, the Court was purporting to apply the Fourteenth Amendment's Due Process Clause, which provides that no state shall "deprive any person of life, liberty, or property, without due process of law." As the term itself implies, due process is about process. But in the law, there's a difference between *procedural* fairness (*e.g.*, whether the parties were given an adequate opportunity to present evidence, make their arguments, and otherwise be heard) and *substantive* fairness (*e.g.*, whether the law imposed burdens that were themselves unfair, regardless of any procedural improprieties). And yet in *Lochner*, the Court invalidated the law at issue not because of any *procedural* unfairness, but rather because the Court considered the law indefensible for *substantive* reasons, based on its own assessment that "[t]here is no reasonable ground for interfering with the liberty of person or the right of free contract, by determining the hours of labor, in the occupation of a baker."

Because it focuses on the substance of the law rather than procedural fairness—and because it is said to be rooted in the Fourteenth Amendment's to act under the Due Process Clause—the type of reasoning employed in *Lochner* has become known as "substantive due process." If you find this approach sketchy, unsettling, and capable of all kinds of mischief, you're not alone. I'm right there with you.

As a conservative, I tend to believe that governments are not well-equipped to establish wages and hours for workers. In my view, free-market forces are far better suited for such tasks. But nothing in the Constitution prohibits the states from embracing a different view in their laws. By pretending otherwise, five justices in *Lochner* cynically substituted their own (conservative) policy preferences for the (progressive) policy choices embodied in a New York statute—one that by all accounts had been properly enacted by a duly elected legislature in that state. They did so, moreover, in a way that turned on the Court's own, subjective assessment of a law's reasonableness, and then equating that ruling with the Constitution itself. Conservative policy victory or not, this was a bad ruling and a loss for the Constitution.

But let's get back to 1905. After the *Lochner* ruling, a narrative began to emerge of so-called "conservative" jurists—including Associate Justices Rufus Peckham and Joseph McKenna—against more liberal members like Associate Justices Oliver Wendell Holmes and Louis Brandeis.

But despite these supposed rivalries, which were undoubtedly exaggerated by the political press, on the whole the Court performed its duties quite well during those years. After all, most of the Court's docket had nothing to do with substantive due process or any other attempt to constitutionalize blatantly political issues. So much like today's Supreme Court, the Supreme Court of the early twentieth century was not a bad Court that occasionally did good things. It was a good Court that occasionally did bad things.

Cynically speaking, one could argue that this is a little like saying that "Mrs. Lincoln really enjoyed most of the play," but it really isn't. While not supported by the text and original understanding of the constitutional language in question, the reasoning employed in *Lochner* reflected views shared by many Americans of that era—and even by some modern legal scholars for whom I have great respect. In any event, most of the Court's rulings reflected far more care and caution than even the most critical reading of *Lochner* might suggest.

In hindsight, the *Lochner* era is a good illustration of the Court at work during tumultuous, divisive, and uncertain times. Much like today, when substantive due process has come roaring back with a vengeance—manifesting itself in controversial haymakers like *Roe* v. *Wade*—the Supreme Court did a lot of good when it wasn't trying to resolve political disputes, venturing far outside the scope of its judicial power. Those years, like our time, saw nine justices—all from different backgrounds and carrying sometimes divergent legal philosophies—interpreting the law to the best of their abilities and reaching decisions based on what they concluded. In some cases, these nine justices ruled in what you might call a "conservative" direction, and in other cases, they remained relatively "liberal."

Importantly, however, at no point during this era was it seriously suggested that additional justices be added to the Court for the purpose of achieving different outcomes; nor would any of the justices have admitted that any political beliefs drove their decisions. And, as always, most of the opinions they reached during those years were unanimous, even

amidst the rapid ascendance of the industrial age as a domi-
nant force in American life—something that had completely
changed the sorts of cases that the Court heard on any given
day.

Despite its errors and the flaws of its members, the
Supreme Court was admired, respected, and generally deemed
to have the country's best interests at heart.

Oddly, however, the Court wouldn't have its own building
until 1935. After spending the first two decades of the republic
meeting in taverns, basement offices, and private homes, the
Court set up shop in (what is now considered) the basement
of the Capitol—first in a committee room starting in 1801,
and then in a chamber (patterned after the Temple of Posei-
don) specifically designed for the Court's use beginning in
1810, where it would remain (with a brief interruption resulting from damage caused by British troops during the War of
1812) until 1860.

In 1860, the Court moved upstairs into the chamber that
had previously been occupied by the United States Senate.

It was in those quarters that the Court began to flex its
judicial muscles more than ever before. It wasn't the location
of the Court that brought about this change as much as it
was the expansion of federal power that resulted from the
so-called "Civil War Amendments" to the Constitution, especially the Fourteenth Amendment. The Fourteenth Amendment imposed significant restrictions on the states, expressly
prohibiting them from denying U.S. citizens equal protection

under the law or depriving them of life, liberty, or property without due process. The Fourteenth Amendment's Due Process Clause in particular was interpreted by the Supreme Court to make most of the protections in the Bill of Rights— which originally imposed restrictions only on the *federal* government—binding on the states. This understanding of the Fourteenth Amendment, which is commonly known as the "incorporation doctrine," started to gain momentum in the late 1890s, and was in full swing by the time *Lochner* was decided in 1905. In fact, without the Fourteenth Amendment and the incorporation doctrine, a case like *Lochner* would never have reached the Supreme Court (or any federal court, for that matter), because the Constitution would not have been implicated.

Stated simply, after the ratification of the Fourteenth Amendment, there were far more ways in which a state law could be deemed to violate the Constitution. And once *Lochner* became a thing, the Supreme Court's prominence as a venue for challenging state laws escalated dramatically. According to a recent study of the matter, during this era, "the number of state statutes invalidated by the U.S. Supreme Court jumped from less than one per decade prior to the Civil War to more than three per decade at the end of the nineteenth century to nearly one per year in the thirty years after the *Lochner* decision."[1]

As the Court's role became more prominent, it naturally became more controversial. Nevertheless, that does not mean that the Court was in charge of everything. In fact, it was for the most part still a relatively quiet and steadying force in American society. And as is true today, it was easy to exaggerate the intensity of any controversy surrounding the Court and its role in our system of government.

"Most of the important legislative measures that were really demanded by public opinion," writes Robert McCloskey of the period, "did pass and did manage to survive the gauntlet of judicial review."[2]

But beginning with *Lochner*, an ideological war regarding the federal judiciary was underway. The battle lines, which concerned the balance of power between states and the federal government—and between the three branches of the federal government—were being drawn. All the Court needed to begin the fight was a villain—a president willing to expand the federal government (and the executive branch in particular) beyond where the Court believed it should go.

During the 1912 election cycle, that villain appeared.

———•———

From a young age, Woodrow Wilson was obsessive about order. He loved to organize people, and he often wrote laws for fun.

According to his biographer, A. Scott Berg, one of Wilson's main hobbies as a young man was joining clubs—not so much for the activities around which those clubs were organized, but for the chance to run them. Once he had been admitted as a member, he would propose new rules and regulations, often driving the other members mad. If a club he was joining didn't have some kind of a constitution, he would write one; if the club *did* have a constitution, he would rip it up and rewrite it.

"It became further evident," writes Berg in a section about the young Wilson's time on a baseball team called the Lightfoots, "that his interest in social activities accorded with his ability to run them…There was a schedule for fines: a nickel for swearing, two and a half cents for lesser vulgarities; and absences [from team meetings] cost a dime."[3]

This knack for meddling in the affairs of others was a skill that Wilson carried with him throughout his life. It was present during his schooling and, later, it showed up in the administrations of several colleges where he worked. Born in the South, Wilson had attended Princeton University and exceled in classes on politics and government. As a young man, he made it halfway through law school (he had that in common with another future president who would go on to have trouble with the Supreme Court) and then quit, electing to pursue a doctorate in political science at Johns Hopkins University instead. From there, he became a professor at several of the nation's top universities, always advocating for the progressive cause on campus.

To date, Woodrow Wilson is the only PhD ever to hold the presidency. But that's not what makes him interesting. What makes him interesting, I believe, is that by the time he began his run for the White House in 1911, Wilson had become almost openly contemptuous of the United States Constitution. In some sense, he is the first president of the United States of whom this can be said—although he certainly would not be the last.

Looking back, the future president's ideas about the separation of powers and federal rulemaking abilities were grim harbingers of the regulatory state that was to come. But in those days, he was quieter about it—or, rather, he hid his disdain for the Constitution under a mountain of boring academic prose, outlining his thoughts in long articles in journals such as *Political Science Quarterly*. At the time, it would have been hard for most people to work out the twisted vision that he had for the future of the American republic.

But for anyone who actually read these articles, the message was clear. Wilson, by now a radical progressive, believed that the balance of power as established by the United States Constitution was not quite good enough for the changing circumstances of American citizens in the twentieth century. He believed that we needed to take desperate measures in order to change it. Given the chance, it seemed, he would do exactly that.

In 1887, for instance, he had written a paper, now infamous, titled "The Study of Administration." In it, he argued that the American system of government should function more like a university, with unelected bureaucrats running most of the daily functions rather than elected officials. The "administrative state," as it would come to be known, should be insulated from politics. The experts in charge of governing, according to this theory, should be free to govern as they deem fit—free of the meddling influence of whimsical voters.

"Most important to be observed," he wrote, in a typically opaque sentence, "is the truth already so much and so fortunately insisted upon by our civil service reformers; namely, that administration lies outside the proper sphere of *politics*. Administrative questions are not political questions. Although politics sets the tasks for administration, it should not be suffered to manipulate its offices."[4]

In effect, Wilson was calling for a government very much like the one we have today: thousands of unelected people making key legislative and executive decisions, the vast majority of whom are insulated from democratic choice.

But most Americans at the time did *not* read academic journals like *Political Science Quarterly*, where that article first appeared. And why would they? They were providing for their families, doing their jobs, and trying to make enough money to survive.

By the middle of the 1911 campaign, it seemed that he might be on course to unseat President William Howard Taft and become the first man from the South to win the White House since 1848. But this was far from a typical American election.

A decade earlier, in 1901, Taft's good friend and fellow Republican Theodore Roosevelt had left office as one of the most beloved presidents of modern times. Governing on a progressive agenda, Roosevelt had won reelection easily, stepping away from the office after two terms only because he believed that it was his duty to do so. But before leaving, he handpicked as his successor a man who had been one of his closest friends for decades: William Howard Taft.

Born in 1857 and raised in Ohio, Taft had never had any interest in being president of the United States. He was a lawyer, and a good one, who had served as the United States solicitor general under President Benjamin Harrison. Later, he was named governor-general of the Philippines. In letters to friends, Taft compared himself to an "old slow coach," whose true passion was the law; the negative attention of the press that inevitably came with a career in politics left him, as he was to write to his wife, Nellie, "very, very discouraged."[5] His dream was to become chief justice of the United States Supreme Court.

But the nominations never came. Once, during the presidency of Teddy Roosevelt, there was talk of an offer, but Nellie had advised him to turn it down. She had bigger aspirations. In fact, Taft accepted the endorsement of his friend Teddy Roosevelt largely because of encouragement from his wife, and won the White House easily in 1908. But politics hadn't come easily to him. As his first term drew to a close, progressives were upset that he seemed to be working too closely with conservatives, and conservatives were upset that he wasn't doing enough to advance their cause.

Also, in what must have been a painful twist of irony, he spent a large majority of his time appointing *other* people to the Supreme Court, giving away the job that he so desperately wanted for himself to an astounding six people during his single term in the White House. By that point, only George Washington, who, of course, began his presidency with an empty Supreme Court (giving him the chance to fill it entirely with his own nominees), had left more of an impact on the makeup of the Supreme Court than William Howard Taft. One of Taft's nominees was a lawyer from Wyoming named Willis Van Devanter, who would remain on the Court for 27 years. Another was a famous politician named Charles Evans Hughes, who had been the governor of New York at the time. Eventually, these two men would participate in some of the most heated disputes in the Supreme Court's history.

Personal tragedy had struck as well. In 1909, Nellie Taft had a severe stroke, which left her paralyzed. Now busy caring for her while managing the heavy burdens of the presidency, Taft started showing signs of severe stress. He gained a large amount of weight, topping out at approximately 320 pounds. This was the era when, according to one rumor, Taft somehow got stuck in the White House bathtub. He also grew despondent about his work.

In the midst of all that chaos, in 1910, Teddy Roosevelt returned from a long safari in Africa and decided to take the White House back from the man he'd handed it to years earlier. Their friendship, in effect, had ended. For Taft, who knew that he would never be able to compete with a beloved figure such as Roosevelt in the presidential election, this betrayal by his friend was deeply upsetting.

With the Republican ticket split down the middle, Woodrow Wilson was able to sail easily to victory. He campaigned on a promise to adapt the federal government to suit the needs of a changing nation, taking particular aim at the Constitution. During a campaign speech, he uttered a phrase that would come to define the so-called "living Constitution" theory of government.

"Society," he said, "is a living organism and must obey the laws of life, not of mechanics; it must develop. All that progressives ask or desire is permission—in an era when 'development,' 'evolution,' is the scientific word—to interpret the Constitution according to the Darwinian principle; all they ask is recognition of the fact that a nation is a living thing and not a machine."[6] To Wilson, this "development" or "evolution" meant being able to change or circumvent the Constitution without going through the necessarily difficult process of amending it.

After his victory, Wilson entered the White House and began filling his administration with people who shared his vision for a government run by bureaucratic experts. But their efforts were interrupted by the onset of the Great War (what we now call World War I). During that war, the role of the federal government became far more prominent—not because Wilson willed it to be so with his progressive visions, but because the federal government (being in charge of national defense) necessarily gains prominence in times of war. And while Wilson still had his eye on an aggressive domestic agenda, both the Constitution and World War I stood in his way.

As soon as the United States entered the war, in fact, Wilson's ideas about how the government at home should function became much less important than defeating our enemies abroad. For a while, the confrontation between the conservatives on the Supreme Court and progressives in the other two branches was averted.

The war did, however, bring many of the nation's top progressives to Washington. Many of them had been toiling away in academia for the previous few years, and believed that it was now their duty to help the United States win the war. Others were the sons of wealthy families who saw the war as their chance to work in the White House for a few years. Among the latter group was Franklin Delano Roosevelt, fifth cousin of Theodore Roosevelt, the former president.

At the age of 30, Franklin Roosevelt left his position in the New York State Senate to come to Washington, to serve as the assistant secretary of the Navy. It was a big job for someone so young, and there is no doubt that his name and the connections he'd made in New York politics and as a student at Harvard University helped him.

While working in the Wilson administration, Roosevelt met someone who would become a lifelong friend and a willing accomplice during his later fight to bend the Supreme Court to his will: Felix Frankfurter. At the time, Frankfurter was a respected legal scholar who had, by the age of 32, become the first Jewish law professor at Harvard. As a young man, according to the historian Noah Feldman, the author of *Scorpions*, Frankfurter believed that "the conservative Supreme Court of the period had overstepped its authority when it reversed progressive state and federal laws that limited working hours, protected workplace health and safety, and established minimum wages."[7] The Court, in Frankfurter's view, should not have limited the federal government's power to regulate commerce between states, and it did not have much business declaring state labor laws unconstitutional, either.

Frankfurter's criticism seems to focus on two types of decisions. He disagreed with the Court's refusal to interpret the Commerce Clause broadly enough to allow Congress to enact laws governing local activities like labor, manufacturing, agriculture, and mining (which had always been subject to state authority, not federal). He also took issue with the Court's inclination to invalidate state labor laws as it had in *Lochner*, using substantive due process. These two categories of Court decisions were easy enough for experts to differentiate, but among most of the Court's critics they could easily be lumped together, since both were understood as impediments to the progressive agenda.

Fortunately, as a bureaucrat in Woodrow Wilson's War Department, Frankfurter was not yet in a position to do anything about this. That would come later. During his time in that department, all he managed to do was make friends with a young Franklin Delano Roosevelt, who would later call on him constantly for advice about the law. In the years to come, according to Feldman, Frankfurter would make friends with some of the Court's other liberal luminaries, most prominently Associate Justice Louis Brandeis, whose causes he would champion once Brandeis was on the Court and unable to do it himself. He also called for the United States to recognize the Soviet Union, which put him further to the left than even some of his most progressive colleagues were willing to go. By the time his friend Franklin Delano Roosevelt won the presidency, Frankfurter would be described by his friends as "the most influential single individual in the United States."[8]

After the war, Frankfurter toiled away once again as a professor at Harvard, developing the legal theories that would eventually convince *President* Franklin Delano Roosevelt to undertake an effort to pack the Court with liberal justices. Meanwhile, President Woodrow Wilson fell short of implementing plans to create the vast regulatory state that he had envisioned during his years as a professor.

To the surprise of many, the Supreme Court garnered less public attention while Wilson was president than it had a decade earlier. For whatever set of reasons—including many attributable to the war effort, which distracted Wilson from his domestic agenda, where he intended to push the constitutional envelope most aggressively—there were simply fewer politically charged cases before the Court than one might have predicted at the outset of Wilson's presidency.

One notable exception was *Hammer* v. *Dagenhart*, 247 U.S. 251 (1918). In that case, the Court rendered a five-to-four decision invalidating the Keating-Owen Child Labor Act, a law enacted by Congress with Wilson's support—as an exercise of Congress's constitutional authority to regulate interstate commerce—prohibiting the interstate shipment of goods produced at: a mine or quarry that had employed workers under the age of 16 within 30 days of the shipment in question; any manufacturing facility that had employed workers under the age of 14 within 30 days of the shipment in question; or at any manufacturing facility that had employed workers between the ages of 14 and 16 within 30 days of the shipment in question, if any such workers had been permitted to work more than eight hours in a day, or more than six days in a week, after 7:00 p.m. or before 6:00 a.m.

The majority reasoned that the statute in question "not only transcends the authority delegated to Congress over commerce, but also exerts a power as to a purely local matter"—specifically, labor laws—"to which the federal authority does not extend." Understanding that limitation, Congress had purported to regulate not the use of child labor itself, but rather the interstate shipment of things produced with such labor. But this, according to the majority, was insufficient to save the law because, "if Congress can thus regulate matters entrusted to local authority by prohibition of the movement of commodities in interstate commerce…the power of the States over local matters may be eliminated, and thus, our system of government be practically destroyed."

Writing for the Court's four dissenting members in that case, Associate Justice Oliver Wendell Holmes noted that the statute in question didn't regulate labor itself, but rather the sale in one state of specified products produced in another state, which is the very definition of interstate commerce. As Holmes explained, "The act does not meddle with anything belonging to the States. They may regulate their internal affairs and their domestic commerce as they like. But when they seek to send their products across the state line, they are no longer within their rights. If there were no Constitution and no Congress, their power to cross the line would depend on their neighbors. Under the Constitution, such commerce belongs not to the States, but to Congress to regulate....Instead of being encountered by a prohibitive tariff at her boundaries, the State encounters the public policy of the United States, which it is for Congress to express."

Child labor is reprehensible, and we can all rest assured that it has for many decades been banned by federal law and in all fifty states. But it's important to remember that the Court was speaking not to whether child labor was a good thing or a bad thing. Nor was it speaking to whether it should be prohibited by law. While this case happened to involve child labor, the main legal question in this case was which government (state or federal) had the authority to act, and thus to make judgment calls regarding the precise contours of such a law. And if you recognize that the statute invalidated in *Hammer* was essentially a labor law, it becomes easier to understand the Court's conclusion that this statute was not an appropriate exercise of Congress's Commerce Clause authority. That power had never been understood to extend to things like labor, manufacturing, agriculture, and mining—things that, while economic, are typically *intra*-state endeavors, and are therefore subject to state law, not federal. While Justice Holmes was right to suggest that Congress would have authority—under the Commerce Clause, no less—to exclude or disfavor products made with child labor in a foreign country, doing so would not undermine the sovereign authority of a state, which federal officials are duty-bound to protect. Excluding from *interstate* commerce products made with child labor in a state that has chosen to allow it, by contrast, would undermine state authority.

Then again, when you look at what that statute actually says—and specifically at the fact that the articles regulated under it are limited to those produced in one state and sold in another, which is the very definition of interstate commerce—it becomes arguable that the Court could have upheld this law. Congress in fact has the power to regulate products made in one state and sold in another, and that's what Congress did when it enacted the Keating-Owen Child Labor Act. Given that the same Supreme Court had upheld other federal laws (also enacted under the Commerce Clause) prohibiting the interstate shipment of everything from lottery tickets to contaminated food and drug products to prostitutes, it's not hard to formulate an argument that the justices comprising the five-member majority in *Hammer* v. *Dagenhart* might have allowed their own political philosophies to impact their reasoning in that case.

On the other hand, none of the laws just mentioned could be said to essentially compel every state—as a matter of economic coercion—to ban even *intra*-state activities involving prostitution, lottery tickets, and contaminated food and drug products. The law invalidated in *Hammer* did have that effect, leaving states no realistic choice but to ban child labor in precisely the manner Congress preferred. That, it appears to me, is the best explanation of the Court's ruling in *Hammer*: it erred on the side of preserving state authority. While modern critics condemn it as turning a blind eye to labor practices that we properly deem barbaric today, it's important to remember that federal law is no less capable of perpetuating (or even inflicting) barbarism than state law. Bad policy can be found in both, and has been throughout our history as a nation. The Constitution protects state authority by limiting federal power, even though state laws sometimes embody bad policy. By so doing, it gives Americans more of the kind of government they want, and less of the kind of government they don't want—clarifying lines of authority, while preserving the rich diversity of viewpoints that exists among and between the states.

In any event, insofar as *Hammer* v. *Dagenhart* was perceived as a politically motivated overreach of judicial authority—as an instance of judicial activism by conservative jurists who simply disliked the policy choice made by Congress in its efforts to end the pernicious scourge of child labor—one could make the case that it cheapened legitimate discussions regarding the outer lim-its of Congress's authority under the Commerce Clause. Even *perceived* deviations from the constitutional text and structure are not without consequence, as they tend to produce overcorrections down the road by justices who, having perceived a wrong, might become more inclined in a future case to use a little too much cowbell in an effort to correct it. That's why it's so important for the Court to speak with unmistakable clarity and precision. To the extent it invalidated a child-labor law without adequately articulating a proper justification for doing so, the majority in *Hammer* may have contributed to an overcorrection by the Court nearly two decades later, when the Court would interpret the Commerce Clause broadly enough to authorize Congress to reg-ulate not only the interstate movement of articles of commerce, but also any endeavor that, broadly speaking, *substantially affects* interstate commerce. But more on that later.

Regardless, *Hammer* v. *Dagenhart* was perhaps the single most significant clash between the Wilson administration and the Court. By the end of Wilson's presidency, it was apparent that the American legal system had emerged intact—in spite of the Court's controversial ruling in *Hammer,* and in spite of President Wilson's longstanding antipathy toward it.

That, of course, would not be the case forever.

—————

Meanwhile, not long after President Wilson had assumed office, William Howard Taft had relocated to New Haven,

Connecticut, where he took a professorship at Yale Law School. He did not believe that his career was over, necessarily, but he knew that a seat on the Supreme Court was unlikely. He was content, it seemed, to live out his postpresidency on the campus of Yale, writing about the law and teaching eager, young law students. For a man who had always enjoyed quiet contemplation of the law more than the rush and clamor of politics, this seemed like a great fit.

Then, in December, he got a call from President Warren G. Harding, whom Taft had supported during Harding's 1920 campaign. Harding said that he wanted to meet with Taft at his home in Ohio to discuss potential appointments. Taft went to see him. Upon his arrival, Taft learned that there would soon be vacancies to fill on the Supreme Court. But Taft, given his experience as president and with the Court, knew that there would be problems. As president, Taft had nominated two of the justices with whom he would now be serving, and he had opposed the nomination of Louis Brandeis. It would be improper, Taft believed, to take a position as an associate justice given the circumstances. The only job he would accept—indeed, the only one that he *could* accept according to the norms of the Court—was the one he had longed for as a young man: *chief* justice.

A few months later, the offer finally came. After a quick confirmation in the Senate (which was still the norm at the time), he was sworn in as Chief Justice William Howard Taft on June 30, 1921, becoming the only man to have served both as the president of the United States and the chief justice of the Supreme

Court. Given the increasingly partisan nature of the presidency, it is difficult to imagine anyone ever holding both jobs again.

During his time as chief justice, Taft didn't do much to tip the Court's ideological balance. For the most part, the relationship between the Court and the other two branches of government remained the same, seeing only occasional battles over the constitutionality of laws, which, in a sense, were indications of the large fight that was to come during the New Deal era. In hindsight, the reign of Taft seems very much like the calm before a terrible storm.

But Chief Justice Taft did make one enormous contribution to the Supreme Court, one that has had more of an impact on the Court's public appearance than any opinion he could have written or any legal precedent he could have set. Early in his term as chief justice, Taft went down the hall to the Senate chamber to ask Congress to appropriate funds to build the first permanent home for the Supreme Court.

According to Taft's testimony, he had in mind a grand structure—something that would inspire awe in all who approached the Court. Congress approved his plan, and quickly began working with Cass Gilbert, an architect who had designed several of the most prominent skyscrapers in the world at the time, on the plans. Luckily, Gilbert had a similarly high opinion of the Court, once calling it "the greatest tribunal in the world, one of the three great elements of our national government."[9]

But there was a problem.

The space that Congress had allotted for the Court in 1932

was small, occupying an oddly shaped swath of land in the middle of Washington, DC. For years, an old tavern had stood on the land. During the Civil War, it had been converted into a prison for captured Confederate soldiers and spies. In the years since, it became an office building, a tavern again, and then, finally, the headquarters of the National Women's Party. By the time the rubble was cleared and the dirt was carted away, Gilbert realized that he had a relatively small piece of land to work with. Unlike the nation's other monuments, the Court's building would not have a grand processional or a wide lawn on either side.

So, rather than building out, he decided to build up.

Over a period of years, Gilbert began to incorporate steps into his rough sketches of the Court. *Lots* of them. Eventually, he and Chief Justice Taft settled on the design of the building as we know it today: a grand white hall fronted by eight massive columns of solid marble, all of it sitting high above the rest of our nation's capital. The cornerstone was laid on October 13, 1932, by Charles Evans Hughes, one of the justices Taft had appointed to the Supreme Court, and who had taken Taft's place as chief justice when he died.

"The republic endures," Hughes said, "and this is the symbol of its faith."[10]

Although it was considered overly grandiose by some, for the most part the reception was warm, especially among legal scholars. When they moved into the new building in 1935, the United States Supreme Court officially entered the modern era—and, as the Court's nine justices surely knew, a fight for its very survival.

CHAPTER FOUR

FDR and the Four Horsemen

D UE TO THE TWENTIETH AMENDMENT'S RATIFICATION in 1933, the presidential inauguration of 1937 was held not in March—as it had been for more than 150 years—but in January. In Washington, DC, January is not a great time to plan an outdoor event because it tends to be cold. Really cold.

During floor debates on the amendment a few years earlier, some senators had raised concerns about the potential for bad weather. They knew that snow, sleet, and rain were far more likely in January, and that early winter winds in the capital had a way of chilling people to the bone. But for the most part, their concerns were pushed aside, primarily by Senator George Norris of Nebraska, who had proposed the amendment and was dead set on getting it passed. Four years later, the critics turned out to be right.

By late morning on January 20, 1937, the air was frigid, and rain had been falling for five hours. The streets were flooded, and there had been enough precipitation to soak a top hat and bleed right through the cloth of a down coat. But the crowds that had turned out to hear Franklin Delano Roosevelt speak didn't seem to care. The people—men, women, and children of all ages among them—had lined up all morning, standing in the thick mud of the national mall with their umbrellas held high, their overcoats slung over their heads like makeshift tarps. (Senator Norris, of course, was up in the congressional section, which was protected by a roof.)

But all those present, elected officials and civilians alike, had come out in the rain that day for the same reason: to hear the second inaugural address of a man who, just two months earlier, had won the biggest landslide victory in the history of the United States.

Even to Roosevelt, a man who had never been accused of modesty, the results had been staggering. After just a few hours of voting on Election Day, he had emerged as the clear victor over Alf Landon, the former governor of Kansas whose name, tellingly, is hardly ever spoken anymore. Not only had Roosevelt won just over 60 percent of the popular vote, but almost the entirety of the Electoral College as well.[1]

Given that the Democratic Party also controlled Congress at the time, it's no surprise that Roosevelt felt vindicated—and, in some sense, politically invincible. Throughout his first term, which had begun in the depths of the Great Depression, Roosevelt and his administration had worked hard to give the people what they wanted. At the time, that meant a whole lot of legislation intended to get the economy up and running again, albeit at a huge cost to taxpayers, personal liberty, and constitutionally limited government. For the most part, his programs, a loose package of social legislation that had been dubbed "the New Deal," involved bills that put many functions previously performed automatically by market forces in the hands of the federal government—*i.e.*, in *his* hands.

There was no denying that these programs had brought relief to some Americans, at least for a little while. By the morning of Roosevelt's second inauguration, the economy was beginning to recover. There were people getting back to work. But no one was quite sure how long it would last, or what the long-term effects of this legislation would be. To many, they represented a gross overreach by the federal government, which had become something closer to a dictatorship during the New Deal era. Roosevelt was accumulating power by expanding the functions of government, federalizing many functions of government that had historically (and constitutionally) been reserved for the states. And he was consolidating that power firmly in the executive branch, allowing it to take over many fundamentally legislative functions, which are supposed to be performed only by Congress. While some Americans welcomed these changes, others saw them as threats to the text and structure of our Constitution.

Some of the most prominent figures in the latter camp happened to serve on the Supreme Court, and they had been frustrating Roosevelt's plans for a complete government takeover for as long as he had been in office. Naturally, they had been invited to the inauguration, too.

That morning, at precisely eleven o'clock, the justices donned their robes and entered their chambers just as they might have on any other Tuesday in January. Then, without delay, Chief Justice Charles Evans Hughes announced that the justices would be departing their new home in the Supreme Court building and heading out into the rain to watch the inauguration.

It would have been hard to say no, even if they'd wanted to. According to accounts from friends and colleagues, Chief Justice Hughes was a commanding presence. Robert Jackson, with whom Justice Hughes would later serve for a few years on the Court, once wrote that Hughes "looks like God and talks like God."[2] But two justices had said no, at least in effect. Associate Justice Louis Brandeis, a stalwart liberal and an acquaintance of President Roosevelt's, made a point never to appear at public events, and he was making no exception for the inauguration. Associate Justice Harlan Fiske Stone, who had taken ill some months earlier, was still recovering and would also be absent.

Shortly after 11:00 a.m., the remaining seven justices removed their black robes and folded them into boxes, and then handed those boxes to messengers who'd come across town for the sole purpose of carrying them. The robes of Supreme Court justices are, by the way, the only form of ceremonial clothing used at the highest levels of American government, and are supposed to be handled with great respect.

The justices were then escorted to the basement of the new Supreme Court building and packed into black cars, which would take them to the Capitol, which is literally across the street. Although the Capitol and the Supreme Court are separated by only a few hundred feet, that drive must have felt like a trip back in time. These seven justices had all worked in a relatively small room down the hall from the Senate chamber earlier in their careers, moving across the street to their new chambers on April 12, 1935—less than two years before Franklin D. Roosevelt's second inauguration. Most of them had spent most of their Supreme Court careers working at the Capitol, and before the Court had become an institution fraught with so much controversy, and when it seemed that the days of adding seats to the Court (and fighting about it along partisan, political lines) were long over, relegated to the nineteenth century where they belonged.

This morning, things were different. The man who was set to give his second inaugural address had been preparing for years to declare war on the Court, but his intentions had been kept mostly behind the scenes. There were rumors that he would use the address to fire the first shot in this war, letting the Supreme Court know that it had to get in line or face the consequences.

Those who followed events in Washington would understand why. For years, the Roosevelt administration had watched while the Supreme Court struck down many of his signature New Deal programs in rapid succession. In most instances, the Court had acted based on a conclusion that the legislation at issue violated one (or sometimes both) of the Constitution's core "structural" protections: the "vertical" protection of federalism, rooted in the premise that the authority of the federal government is narrow and limited to functions designated as federal in the Constitution, with all other powers of government reserved to the states "or to the people"; and the "horizontal" protection known as "separation of powers," specifying that within the federal government, the legislative branch (Congress) makes the law, the executive branch (headed by the president) enforces the laws, and the judicial branch (headed by the Supreme Court) resolves disputes as to the proper interpretation of the laws. Both of these protections—federalism and separation of powers—had been carefully designed to work in tandem to protect the American people against the risks inherent in the dangerous accumulation of government power in the hands of the few.

Unfortunately for Roosevelt, and for the American people, the president's New Deal ambitions would *require* the unprecedented accumulation of power in the hands of the few, implicating both federalism and separation of powers.

In previous eras of American history, presidents and members of Congress alike had been sufficiently protective of these core constitutional protections to prevent their usurpation. That cautious inclination within the two political branches waned considerably during Roosevelt's presidency, when the progressive impulse to "do something" in response to the Great Depression—coupled FDR's popularity and substantial Democratic majorities in both the House and

Senate—led to an era of extreme deference to a president who was determined to upset the constitutional order.

Thus, the only thing left standing in his way at this point was the Supreme Court—the head of the one branch of government that is not immediately subject to the political forces of the day, and over which the president has no control, beyond his power to fill vacancies with the advice and consent of the Senate. That is precisely what led to Roosevelt's desire to create additional vacancies on the Court—vacancies that, once filled by him, would make the Court less likely to oppose him. While not every member of the Court agreed, enough of them did that it created problems for Roosevelt.

To understand the dynamics at play in the Court during that era, it can be helpful to divide the nine justices serving at the time into three groups. The largest group consisted of the Court's conservatives. Dubbed "the Four Horsemen" by the press (a reference to the biblical "Four Horsemen of the Apocalypse"), this group was known for its staunch opposition to the New Deal effort to expand the size and scope of the federal government. (The fact that the press settled on this derisive term—apparently to denigrate members of the Court daring to question FDR's wisdom and check his aggressive quest to empower himself— probably tells us something about the political leanings of the American news media establishment, which has long glorified efforts by their fellow progressives to empower the federal government.) The Four Horsemen consisted of Associate Justices Pierce Butler (nominated by President Harding in 1922),

James McReynolds (nominated by President Wilson in 1914), George Sutherland (nominated by President Harding in 1922), and Willis Van Devanter (nominated by President Taft in 1910).

The liberal counterparts to the Four Horsemen, known to some as the "Three Musketeers," included Associate Justices Louis Brandeis (nominated by President Wilson in 1916), Benjamin Cardozo (nominated by President Hoover in 1932), and Harlan Fiske Stone (nominated by President Coolidge in 1925, although he would later be nominated to become chief justice by FDR in 1941).

That unique lineup—between four staunch conservatives (only three of whom had been nominated by Republicans) and three committed liberals (only one of whom had been nominated by a Democrat)—led to many close cases being decided by the Court's two moderates. That group included Chief Justice Charles Evans Hughes and Associate Justice Owen Roberts, both of whom had been nominated by Republican President Herbert Hoover in 1930. That meant that, as long as either Hughes or Roberts agreed with the Four Horsemen in a close, politically charged case, the conservative position would almost certainly prevail. Roberts was generally regarded as the more conservative of the two, so in many instances he was the deciding vote.

That is precisely what happened in the 1936 case *Carter* v. *Carter Coal Company*, when Justice Roberts joined the Four Horsemen in voting to invalidate the Bituminous Coal

Conservation Act of 1935, which imposed sweeping federal regulations on the coal industry, regulating everything from labor standards to competition policy—all pursuant to Congress's authority to regulate interstate commerce under Article I, Section 8, Clause 3 of the Constitution. The majority concluded (correctly in my view) that, although coal production is an economic activity that has countless interstate ramifications, that doesn't mean Congress is free to regulate it comprehensively. As explained by the majority in *Carter*, Congress's authority to regulate interstate commerce does not encompass the power to regulate activities that, while economic in nature, take place in one state at one time—endeavors like labor, manufacturing, agriculture, and mining. The justices explained that "commodities produced or manufactured within a state are intended to be sold or transported outside the state does not render their production or manufacture subject to federal regulation under the commerce clause." The Court described as "inescapable" the conclusion that: "the effect of the labor provisions of the [Bituminous Coal Conservation Act], including those in respect of minimum wages, wage agreements, collective bargaining, and the Labor Board and its powers, primarily falls upon production and not upon commerce; and confirms the further resulting conclusion that production is a purely local activity. It follows that none of these essential antecedents of production constitutes a transaction in or forms any part of interstate commerce. Everything which moves in interstate commerce has had a local origin.

Without local production somewhere, interstate commerce, as now carried on, would practically disappear. Nevertheless, the local character of mining, of manufacturing and of crop growing is a fact, and remains a fact, whatever may be done with the products."

The Three Musketeers dissented. Chief Justice Hughes issued a separate opinion that, while concurring in the judgment, largely agreed with the reasoning of the Court's liberals.

On other occasions, both Hughes and Roberts joined the Four Horsemen, producing a series of six-to-three victories for conservatives in cases involving key New Deal programs. That happened in *United States* v. *Butler*, 297 U.S. 1 (1936), when both Hughes and Roberts voted with the Four Horsemen to strike down the Agricultural Adjustment Act of 1933, with the Three Musketeers dissenting.

It is perhaps ironic that a major early salvo of the Court's war on the New Deal had been fired by all the justices acting together. On May 27, 1935, a day that would come to be known as "Black Monday," the Court had handed down three decisions that damaged New Deal programs, including the vaunted National Industrial Recovery Act (NIRA). At a press conference a few days later, Roosevelt called the NIRA ruling "one of the most important decisions ever rendered in this country" and groused that his government had "been relegated to the horse-and-buggy definition of interstate commerce."[3] All three of the decisions rendered on "Black Monday" had been unanimous. But as the years went on and the New Deal fights continued, the divisions between the "Four Horsemen" and "Three Musketeers" became more defined.

New Deal supporters, in the White House, the press, and elsewhere, argued that the justices were ruling against Roosevelt's legislation because of some inherent conservatism of the Court—in other words, that the Four Horsemen were acting according to their personal politics, not fealty to the Constitution. But that, at least according to the later writings of Chief Justice Charles Evans Hughes, was incorrect. The reason that they were ruling against the Roosevelt administration's bills, he would write later, is that the bills were sloppily written.

Washington typically puts aside these conflicts to mark traditional celebrations, and the 1937 inauguration was no exception. When the justices reached the Capitol to take part in inaugural ceremonies, they got out of their cars and entered the Senate chamber, where they waited out the rain and awaited their robes. For a moment, according to *The New York Times*, the messengers who had brought them over from the Supreme Court building were held up at the door of the chamber, apparently unable for the moment to gain the proper security clearances.[4] But that was soon sorted out, and the justices made their way outside with their robes on their backs.

There had been rumors swirling during the past year, none of them quite substantiated, that Roosevelt had a plan— one that would allow him to control not just the executive branch and Congress, but the Supreme Court, too. He and his close aides in the White House had observed that many of the decisions against them had come down to a close vote of either five-to-four or six-to-three, with the Four Horsemen and some combination of Chief Justice Hughes and Associate Justice Roberts (sometimes both) voting to invalidate his New Deal legislation on constitutional grounds. So, he figured, what he needed was not better legislation, but a few more justices—presumably, jurists would see the Constitution the way he did, as an obstacle to executive power rather than a document of laws that should be followed.

He would, according to the rumors, enlarge the Court from nine members to fifteen, ensuring that nearly all future decisions would go his way. No one was quite sure how he had planned to do this, or what justification he would use when he did. But they were sure about one thing: if he did stuff the Court with new justices, then those justices would be beholden to him. They would be much more willing to support his programs, even those that plainly violated the Constitution and vested far too much power in the federal government.

It would make him an American strongman of sorts, in control of all three branches of government. And depending on what newspapers you read, that might have been his goal all along.

But there were obstacles, even for a leader as beloved as Roosevelt. For one thing, public opinion was against him. The very notion of Court packing, or a partisan judiciary in general, was believed to be politically toxic at the time. Back then, saying that a Supreme Court justice had anything other than a detached, impartial view of the law was akin to saying that he had a criminal record. It simply was not done. So, when Roosevelt, speaking during a late campaign stop in Minnesota, had suggested (rather tamely, in hindsight) that the Court "in particular" was to blame for the lack of progress in the country, and that it was "controlled" by the Republican Party, he was lambasted in the press for speaking about the Court as a political, rather than a judicial, branch of government.[5]

Writing in an editorial, *The Washington Post* demanded that he "immediately withdraw the insult" to the Supreme Court.[6] For a while, reactions of that sort had seemed to dissuade him, at least in public. But no one had any illusions that President Roosevelt, a man not known for changing his mind once it was made up, would give up on the idea for long, least of all the seven justices who had gathered in the teeming rain to hear his second inaugural address. This, they surely knew, was a man who had overcome a deadly, often-debilitating illness to become governor of New York and then president of the United States.

He had, in other words, an iron will. If there was something standing in the way of what he wanted, he would do everything he could to destroy that thing. And in this case, the thing standing between Roosevelt and what he wanted—total control of the United States—was a fair, independent judiciary, and the members of that judiciary knew it.

For the justices, the question was not *whether* he would attack, but *when*. As the six associate justices present that day watched Chief Justice Hughes stride up to the podium carrying the Roosevelt family Bible, wrapped carefully in cellophane to keep it safe from the weather, they wondered what might pass unspoken between the two men.

Seconds later, Roosevelt joined Hughes, and the crowd fell silent, leaving only the sound of rain falling on uncovered heads and shoulders. In the time between Roosevelt's arrival and the beginning of the ceremony, according to newspapers, his hat had been soaked; so, too, had the hat of his wife, Eleanor, who sat right in front. By the time Chief Justice Hughes began speaking, most everyone who'd come that afternoon was similarly uncomfortable.

But the ceremony was captivating enough to make them forget it. As Chief Justice Hughes uttered the words of the presidential oath of office, articulating each syllable clearly in his smooth, commanding baritone, a laminated flag rose slowly up a flagpole behind them. It was an arresting image, especially given the bad weather.

Then the chief justice paused, awaiting Roosevelt's response.

It was then that Roosevelt did something strange, albeit rather subtle. Rather than simply replying *I do*, as was customary at the time, he repeated the entire oath back to Chief Justice Hughes, placing special emphasis on certain words: "I do solemnly swear (or affirm) that I will faithfully execute the Office of President of the United States, and will to the best of my ability, *preserve, protect and defend* the *Constitution* of the United States."

He had sent a message after all, only not in explicit words. But it didn't go unnoticed by the justices, or by the crowd. On the front page of the next day's *New York Times*, a political reporter wrote that the oddly emphasized oath was "a moment to be remembered. One might say that it was not so much what was said as the way in which it was said."[7]

For the rest of the afternoon, Roosevelt did not make any explicit mention of the Supreme Court or its members. He did not, in fact, refer to the judicial branch at all, saying only that all three branches needed to come together to meet the moment.

In later years, it was revealed that Roosevelt had indeed made plans to include a few words about the Court in his address. But he had decided to strike these lines at the last minute, preferring to save the fight for a few weeks after his inauguration.

His plan to pack the Court—and there *was* such a plan; there had been, in fact, for many months now—had been secret for a long time, and it would remain secret for a few weeks more.

But only for a few weeks.

From the moment President Roosevelt had begun discussing the prospect of Court packing, he had demanded that the plan be kept as secret as possible. He knew as well as anyone that having such a thing go public, especially during an election that he still believed he could lose, would be politically disastrous. So he and a small group of aides worked in secret.

By the time he delivered his second inaugural address, fewer than ten people had learned about it. In a normal city, that would have been considered a secret pretty well kept. But in Washington, DC, where rumors fly like rain on a windy afternoon, it was practically a miracle.

One of these coconspirators was Homer Cummings, the attorney general who'd been with Roosevelt for just under four years. A relatively young lawyer who did not command much respect in legal or political circles of the time, Cummings had been an alternate for the position of attorney general, getting the job only when Roosevelt's first choice for the role died suddenly a few days after he was asked to take it. Cummings was supposed to have served only a few years and then given the job to someone with more experience. But the day of his resignation never came.

During his first years in the Roosevelt administration, Cummings had come to enjoy a close relationship with the president, mostly for his willingness to go along with just about anything Roosevelt wanted. The Court-packing bill is perhaps the clearest illustration of this. While some of the president's other advisors were willing to say no to him on occasion, Cummings had not been inclined to do so.

By the time Roosevelt was elected to office, the country was in a state of distress. The Great Depression was bearing down, and people were desperate. Wages were stagnant, and many people were out of work. All over the nation's capital, tent cities had begun popping up, and things only got worse as you moved farther out in the country. During the campaign, Roosevelt had promised a strong federal response to the Great Depression.

His first term was the time to write those bills, many of which would be sweeping and extremely broad measures that gave the federal government an enormous amount of control over the U.S. economy. For Roosevelt, writing this legislation was no easy task. The new president had never been an adept student of economic policy—or of economics in general. At Harvard University, where he had been admitted largely because of his last name, he had averaged a "Gentleman's C." During law school at Columbia, his academic performance had declined even more precipitously. Professors there described him as an "indifferent law student." Writing a few years later in his memoirs, Robert Jackson—a man Roosevelt would later nominate to the Supreme Court—would write in his reflections on the New Deal writing process that Roosevelt "did not really like the judicial process with its slow movement, its concern with detail, its insistence on primary evidence, its deliberation. He wanted short cuts."[8]

It showed. When it came, the New Deal legislation was sloppy, overly broad, and unfocused. It was as if Roosevelt had taken a few of his college term papers, full of broad generalizations and half-baked notions about government, and then somehow convinced Congress to enact them as the supreme law of the land. As soon as the legislation was enacted, the administration knew that litigation was imminent, and that many of the resulting cases would eventually make their way to the Supreme Court. This is something for which the Justice Department, led by Homer Cummings at the time, should have prepared.

But they didn't. Part of that was sheer incompetence, but for the most part, it was politics. During the president's first term, Cummings had made several promises of patronage jobs to friends and campaign supporters. So had Roosevelt. After the boss was reelected by a wide margin in the election of 1937, the bill on those promises came due. That is how Attorney General Cummings, the chief legal officer within the Roosevelt administration, found himself at the head of a justice department staffed with second-rate lawyers and political appointees. It certainly was not the kind of team you wanted when you were going to do battle in the United States Supreme Court.

By the time Roosevelt took to the podium to deliver his second inaugural address, the New Deal as he had originally conceived it was in shambles. The effect must have seemed strange.

Now more than ever, he had the people at his back, having won almost the entire Electoral College. But as far as legislation went, he was effectively powerless. It was time, he decided, to act.

The only option, it seemed, was to pack the Court.

But the problem of public opinion remained. For nearly 150 years, the Supreme Court had maintained strict independence from the petty business of politics. Its justices, as we have seen, were avatars of the law itself, at least in the public imagination. To begin fiddling around with the Court for nakedly political motives would have been a bridge too far, even for the hardheaded Roosevelt.

So he came up with a kind of cover story.

For years, writers and scholars had raised concerns about the advanced age of the justices. It was true that at the time of Roosevelt's second inauguration, the average age of the members of the Supreme Court was at its highest, up to that point. A few years earlier, two newspaper columnists had written a bestselling book about the justices called *Nine Old Men*, which portrayed the justices as "aloof from all reality, meting out a law as inflexible as the massive blocks of marble that surround them in their mausoleum of justice."[9] If there was any good way to attack the Supreme Court, Roosevelt felt, this was it.

He wasn't the first to think so. During the Constitutional Convention in Philadelphia, several of the founders had raised the possibility of a retirement age for justices, fearing that their mental faculties might decline faster than their ability to realize that something was wrong. But men like Alexander Hamilton argued against the proposition, writing with characteristic flair in *The Federalist*, no. 79, that "the dismission of men from stations in which they have served their country long and usefully, on which they depend for subsistence, and from which it will be too late to resort to any other occupation for a livelihood, ought to have some better apology to humanity than is to be found in the imaginary danger of a superannuated bench."[10]

In the end, Hamilton's side won out, and probably for the best. While it's certainly possible that justices over the age of 75 might not be able to read and write about the law with the same vigor that they once did, the opposite, that they will acquire more knowledge and passion as they age, could also be true. It depends on the person. In the past few years alone, we have seen several members of the Court, including Anthony Kennedy and Stephen Breyer, retire voluntarily, believing it was time for someone else to occupy the seat. In my view, almost anyone who has been so successful in the law will be able to know their own limitations when the time comes.

But in an age in which mixing politics and the Court was nearly impossible, at least for presidents who wanted their approval ratings to remain above water, the age angle was Roosevelt's only shot. He dove in with both feet, all the while acknowledging in private that it was a sham.

But the plan went on as scheduled, its contents known only to a very small group of advisors in the West Wing.

The only hints of what was coming arrived through whispers and anonymous leaks, sometimes from the president himself. A few times during his first and second terms, for instance, President Roosevelt called in a correspondent from *Collier's Magazine* named George Creel and dictated entire articles about the failures of the Supreme Court, which were nearly always published in full the next day.[11] (These, apparently, were the days when the liberal media did not take such great pains to hide the fact that they were essentially the PR arm of the Democratic Party.)

When it became clear that the American public was receptive to what he was writing—or, at least, not dead set against it—Roosevelt's team made plans to announce the Court-packing bill, which would officially be titled the Judicial Procedures Reform Bill of 1937, on February 2, 1937. He knew the effect that it would have, and how many legal scholars, even the most liberal ones, would be against him. In a letter written to Felix Frankfurter on January 15, Roosevelt seemed to acknowledge this: "Very confidentially," he wrote, "I may give you an awful shock in about two weeks. Even if you do not agree, suspend final judgment and I will tell you the story."[12] But he wasn't worried. In fact, according to Jeff Shesol, author of a book-length history of the Court-packing attempt called *Supreme Power*, President Roosevelt "greatly enjoyed the fact that he had [a bomb] to drop" on the unsuspecting justices, especially the four who had given him so much cause for concern and anguish during his first term.[13]

During the last two weeks of January, Roosevelt began to inform a few members of his "Brain Trust" in the White House about what he and Cummings had been up to. They were, according to later accounts, extremely nervous about the plan. They did not believe it would work, and, in the case of one senior aide, were "scared to death" at the prospect.[14] "What terrified him," Shesol writes, "was precisely what delighted Roosevelt: the artfulness, the deviousness, of making the case against the court one of infirmity rather than ideology. When the cloak came off—as the president's men expected it would—Roosevelt's motives would stand exposed and his integrity, they feared, would be in tatters."[15]

But none of them said so, at least not in a way that was convincing to the president or his closest advisors. Roosevelt was on an island, almost entirely alone, and no one was willing to pull him back, not even the aides who were most scared by the plan. During an annual dinner at the White House in late January with seven out of the nine justices—the same seven who had listened to him deliver his second inaugural address, which was curiously absent of any ill words toward them— Homer Cummings, in Shesol's account of the scene, "slid next to Sam Rosenman, FDR's counselor and speechwriter, and whispered, 'I wish this message were over and delivered…I feel too much like a conspirator.'"[16]

Less than two weeks later, on February 2, the message would be delivered, but the ordeal would not be over.

One day before, Roosevelt announced the plan to his

cabinet, reading from a prepared statement for an hour. As a joke, his son, James Roosevelt, had stationed the White House physician at the door in case anyone went into cardiac arrest upon hearing it. This didn't happen, of course. But there was a fair amount of shock.

The next day, Roosevelt sent a draft of the bill to Congress.

The reaction was as damning as it was swift. In a matter of days, it became clear that Roosevelt had gravely miscalculated. Even the newspapers that usually praised him were aghast. The columnist Walter Lipmann, writing to a large audience, called it "a bloodless coup d'état." A letter to the editor of *The New York Times* said: "Congress is already a mere 'rubber stamp.' Make the Supreme Court one and a dictator will reign supreme. Many, unable to read the handwriting already on the wall of Europe…will of course shout, 'Heil, heil.'"[17]

Now, during our increasingly polarized time, comparisons of American politicians to fascists are nauseatingly common. We have come, regrettably, to a point where presidents can hardly make any moves without swift comparisons to Hitler. But at the time that Roosevelt was introducing his Court plan, those horrible figures from history were still very much alive; they and their parties were able to tell us exactly what they thought of what American presidents did. And when it came to Roosevelt's Court-packing plan, no one was more excited than the Nazis.

A few days after the Court-packing plan was announced, correspondents from the Associated Press reported that the

Nazi press was very much in favor of the idea, viewing the president "as a champion of vigorous leadership against 'outworn' methods of government."[18]

It makes sense if you think about it. For what is fascism, really, if not the complete sublimation of all other branches of government by a strong, charismatic executive? In fact, if you study history, you'll find that injecting the Court with politics and ignoring their rulings when you don't like them is very often the first step in a dictator's playbook.

Before the plan was announced, Roosevelt had hoped that he would at least be able to count on Justices Louis Brandeis and Benjamin Cardozo, the two most liberal justices on the Supreme Court. He was, after all, attempting to pack the Court with more justices just like them, guaranteeing that their side would win out for years, perhaps even decades to come. But this, too, was a grave miscalculation.

In counting on the support of the liberal justices, according to the historian Noah Feldman, author of the book *Scorpions*, Roosevelt "badly mistook the judicial personality." The Court-packing plan, writes Feldman, "was anathema to even the more liberal judges on the Court, precisely because it transformed them from independent judges into rubber stamps. To them, Roosevelt's proposal smacked of presidential self-aggrandizement at the expense of the judiciary whom they represented and led."[19]

But despite the stunning lack of support, Roosevelt entered the fight with the full force of his personality, with which—in his mind, at least—he could sell the American people on just about anything. He planned one of his famous fireside chats, scheduled for a few weeks after the announcement, to make the case for the plan. After being convinced that the plan was indeed a good idea, Felix Frankfurter sent extensive notes from Harvard. President Roosevelt also worked cunningly, behind the scenes, promising an eventual Supreme Court seat to an important ally, Senate Majority Leader Joe Robinson of Arkansas, if the man would take up the cause in the Senate.

The plan worked, at least for a while. There were debates in the Senate that seemed to sway a tiny portion of the electorate toward Roosevelt's way of thinking; the fireside chat, which was delivered with Roosevelt's characteristic blend of humor and humility, helped a little as well. But public opinion had so far refused to budge. In the Senate, Joe Robinson put on a fair performance in an attempt to bring his fellow senators over to the side of Court packing. In one important sense, this was strange. Robinson was a judicial conservative, and had been all his life. He had always attempted to defend the Constitution according to what it said. If he *did* end up getting the seat that Roosevelt had promised him, he would almost certainly side with the enemies of the administration rather than liberals like Brandeis and Cardozo.

It was one miscalculation among many. For a while, it seemed as if the Judicial Procedures Reform Bill, as it was popularly known, had been one of the greatest blunders in

American political history. Barring a series of very strange developments in the White House's favor, the bill had virtually no hope of passing. Even if it failed and came back later in some form or another—and if Roosevelt had any say in the matter, it would—it seemed as though the issue had been resolved, at least in the court of public opinion.

Of course, as we have learned during the past few years, strange things do have a way of happening, especially when they count the most.

CHAPTER FIVE

The Switch in Time That Saved Nine

T HE CROWDS BEGAN GATHERING JUST AFTER DAWN. By late morning, they had formed several long, twisting lines that led out to door of the Supreme Court building and around the massive white columns at its front. This was not uncommon on decision days, especially during the height of President Roosevelt's battles with the Court. But on the morning of Monday, March 29, 1937, the lines were especially long, and the people who'd gathered were more anxious than usual.

The fate of the Supreme Court was at stake, and everyone knew it.

The president's Court-packing plan, despite remaining massively unpopular with voters, lawmakers, and the justices themselves (really anyone who wasn't on President Roosevelt's payroll), was somehow gaining steam. Partly, this was the result of the endless media coverage it had received. But there were also, it seemed, people who were genuinely coming around to the idea. The New Deal, they believed, needed to stand. It had been good for them, and they were afraid of going back to the days of the Great Depression. If the justices weren't going to allow that, they reasoned, then maybe it was time for desperate measures.

The first case of the morning, *West Coast Hotel Co.* v. *Parrish*, was the most consequential. It concerned the minimum-wage law in Washington state. In that sense, at least, it was reminiscent of *Lochner* v. *New York*, the case we discussed a few chapters ago in which five conservative justices in 1905 had invalidated a New York statute limiting the hours of bakery workers. The majority opinion reasoned that the law amounted to an "unreasonable, unnecessary and arbitrary interference with the right and liberty of the individual to contract," and therefore violated the Fourteenth Amendment's Due Process Clause. Less than a year earlier, in *Morehead* v. *New York ex rel. Tipaldo*, the Court had applied *Lochner* in striking down a New York minimum-wage law. *Morehead*, in a sense, was part of the impetus for the Court-packing plan in the first place inasmuch as it signaled yet again the Court's general lack of enthusiasm for progressive legislation. Even though *Morehead* had involved a constitutional challenge to state law (as opposed to federal legislation)—and therefore didn't signal certain doom for his federal legislative agenda—Roosevelt believed that the lingering, anti-progressive sentiment on the Court (as reflected in *Morehead*) was enough of a threat to the New Deal that aggressive action was necessary. But if the Court could somehow be persuaded to overturn *Morehead* (along with *Lochner* and the rest of its progeny) in *West Coast Hotel*, then maybe, just maybe, there was hope for the New Deal.

Now, the people who had gathered outside wondered which path the Court would take. Would they continue to follow its prior rulings regarding the right of private parties to negotiate terms and conditions of employment free from state interference? Or would it bow to political pressure from Roosevelt? It seemed clear to most observers that the Four Horsemen—Associate Justices James C. McReynolds, Pierce Butler, George Sutherland, and Willis Van Devanter—would probably not budge. It seemed comparably clear that Chief Justice Charles Evans Hughes, who had been voting reliably with the liberals as of late, probably would vote with the Three Musketeers, Justices Brandeis, Cardozo, and Stone. In truth, the decision came down to whether Justice Owen Roberts, a conservative jurist who had never shown any strong inclination to join the liberals in such cases, would bow to the pressure and switch his vote.

As the marshal spoke his incantation and brought the Court into session, the crowd inside the chamber was hushed. According to contemporary reports, it was filled with legal scholars, politicians, and other influential members of society, all of whom were riveted by the national drama that was unfolding. Many of them surely knew that they were occupying prime real estate, so to speak. That is, for as long as the Supreme Court has existed, only a select few people have been allowed inside its chambers while oral arguments are occurring or opinions are being read. In many ways, the Court's main chamber is one of the most exclusive places in Washington, DC. Cameras are strictly prohibited, as are audio recording devices. To date, only two pictures of the Court in session—one taken at the Court's old headquarters in the Capitol Building, the other in its new home on First Street, both during the tenure of Chief Justice Hughes—have ever surfaced. A few weeks before this argument, one was sold to *Life* magazine for a huge, and as yet undisclosed, sum.

As the justices appeared from behind the red velvet curtain and took their seats, the crowd prepared to see history unfold. In rendering its decision on *West Coast Hotel Co. v. Parrish*, the Court could overturn *Lochner* and its progeny including *Morehead*, upsetting decades of precedent (in my view, bad precedent) and potentially dooming the Court-packing plan for good. Alternatively, it would leave *Lochner* intact and strike down the Washington state minimum-wage law, dealing another harsh blow to progressives and infuriating Roosevelt in a way that would almost certainly give momentum to the Court-packing plan. Either way, the ruling had the potential to speak volumes about the Court's credibility, independence, and future. From the very first words, it was official. The Court was reversing its position on minimum-wage laws, giving FDR exactly what he wanted. At that moment, word began spreading throughout the chamber, going from the prominent lawyers, who understood the vernacular unique to the Court and this case, to the casual spectators, who probably didn't. The news traveled to the crowd outside the chamber and, finally, to the wire reporters at major news organizations, who would soon let the American public know what had occurred.

To progressives of the day, this ruling must have felt like a much-welcomed rainstorm after a prolonged drought, one that could easily develop into a full-blown monsoon. The Supreme Court had turned its back on decades of conservative precedent in *West Coast Hotel*, opening up at least the hope that the ruling might be a good omen for things to come. Later in the day, it would become clear that the enabler of this about-face had been none other than Associate Justice Owen Roberts. It was widely believed at the time (based on strong circumstantial evidence) that Roberts had become so nervous about the prospect of President Roosevelt adding justices to the bench that he had flipped, giving the president the judicial outcome that Roosevelt wanted in exchange for his leaving the Court alone. It may well have been the first (or at least the most prominent) instance in which a president had used bald-faced intimidation tactics—"nice Court you've got there, it'd be a shame if something…happened to it"—on the Supreme Court and gotten what he wanted.

These tactics were clear to the American public. The Supreme Court had given Roosevelt the rulings that he wanted—presumably setting the stage as well for future rulings just like it, all of which (Roosevelt hoped) would prop up the New Deal legislation that he so desperately wanted upheld. There was virtually no reason for the president to follow through on his plot to pack the Court. To do so in the wake of this development would seem like overkill.

There's an old adage: "A stitch in time saves nine." Because it's British in origin, I'll trust the BBC's explanation that it dates back to 1723 and was originally a sewing term. "The idea," say the Brits, "is that sewing up a small rip with one stitch means the tear is less likely to get bigger, and need more—or, well, nine—stitches later on."[1] It warns us to fix a problem as soon as it arises so that more work won't be required to fix it later. But it's not clear when these words were first picked up and adapted to describe the flip-flopping of Owen Roberts as "the *switch* in time that saved nine." People must have just liked the sound of it. Within a few days, though, the phrase was all over the newspapers and magazines. The entire nation knew that the Supreme Court had drastically altered the fate of the nation, probably for the worse.

For Roosevelt, the switch in time was welcome. The Supreme Court was favorably reacting to his threats, and he had reason to hope that, having overruled *Lochner*, the Court—having now come to its senses—would help him refashion our system of government in his image. But beyond sending what he desperately wanted to interpret as a favorable signal, in truth, the first ruling on the morning of March 29, 1937, didn't do much for him at all. The far more important case—and the one that marks in my opinion the *true* "switch in time that saved nine"—was decided weeks later on April 12.

In that case, *NLRB* v. *Jones & Laughlin Steel*, the stakes were much higher, especially for Roosevelt. A few years earlier, Congress had passed the Wagner Act, which had created the National Labor Relations Board and allowed the federal government to regulate labor relations across the nation. In many ways, it was the quintessential piece of New Deal legislation.

The case arose when the newly created NLRB, attempting to flex its regulatory muscle, charged Jones and Laughlin Steel Co., which was one of the largest steel producers in the country, with discriminating against employees for not joining unions. If *this* case went Roosevelt's way, then the federal government would have full regulatory authority over labor unions and other important organizations that dealt with commerce between states.

On the morning of April 12, it did. The Wagner Act was upheld, and the Court redefined the Commerce Clause, giving the federal government the regulatory control that so many progressive presidents had sought to give it for years. The implications were sweeping, given that under this new precedent, Congress (and by extension, the federal government) would be empowered to regulate essentially any and every human endeavor as long as it could properly articulate a "substantial relation" between the activity to be regulated and interstate commerce—even though that activity "may be intrastate in character."

This was a dramatic departure not only from Supreme Court precedent, but from the Constitution itself, which had always been understood to confer only limited, enumerated powers on Congress like national defense while reserving everything else to the states. As James Madison explained in *Federalist 45*, the powers of the federal government are "few and defined," while those reserved to the states are "numerous and indefinite." That was true at the time the Constitution was drafted and ratified, and it remained true until April 12, 1937, when five justices (Chief Justice Hughes, joined by the Three Musketeers and Justice Roberts) would turn that principle on its head.

It's hard to overstate how monumental this change was to our system of government. Had this been adopted as a constitutional amendment, it would have stood out as one of the most sweeping changes ever made to the Constitution. There had, of course, been no effort to adopt a constitutional amendment authorizing this breathtaking expansion of federal power. Nor would that have worked for FDR, given that such an amendment would have taken many years to draft, propose, and ratify, and still never would have received the support of two-thirds of both houses of Congress, let alone three-fourths of the state legislatures. It was, in the end, much easier to convince, threaten, and coerce the Supreme Court to simply reinterpret the Constitution to mean what FDR wanted it to mean. So he did just that. And it worked.

In the White House, President Roosevelt was ecstatic.

But to some trusted voices in Roosevelt's inner circle (particularly those most steeped in the Constitution), the switch was cause for concern. In letters to friends and colleagues, Felix Frankfurter of Harvard Law School—who, despite his inclination toward progressive politics, was a legal scholar and jurist at heart—expressed grave concern that Justice Roberts had voted with Roosevelt out of fear, not principle. On the day after the decision, Frankfurter remarked that he wanted to "look for some more honest profession to enter."[2] Ironically, President Roosevelt would later appoint him to the Supreme Court.

Justice Roberts, Frankfurter believed, was not thinking of the Constitution when he voted, but the possibility that President Roosevelt would come in and add seats to the Court, thereby diluting its power and destroying the principle of judicial independence for decades, perhaps permanently. In a letter to Justice Louis Brandeis around the same time, Frankfurter wrote that the decision was "one of life's bitter-sweets, and the bitter far outweighs the sweet."[3]

The Court's decision in *NLRB* v. *Jones & Laughlin Steel* and its fallout is, in my opinion, by far the most significant consequence of the Roosevelt administration's fight to pack the Court, and not in a positive way. Although the effort to pack the Court fell flat as a legislative matter, it was wildly successful as an effort to intimidate the Court. It was successful, however, in a way that substantially diminished the (previously significant) distinction between state and federal power, severely undermining the "vertical" protection of federalism to this day. Once the Court released these particular demons, it was impossible to contain them, resulting in a dramatic expansion of the size, scope, and cost of the federal government.

The Court's analysis in *Jones & Laughlin Steel* led to another ruling five years later—one that helps demonstrate the sheer breath of Congress's now-expanded authority under the Commerce Clause. In 1942's *Wickard* v. *Filburn*, the Court addressed a dispute involving an Ohio wheat farmer named Roscoe Filburn, who dared to challenge the constitutionality of heavy fines he had been ordered to pay by the Secretary of Agriculture. Filburn's offense was egregious under the New Deal rules: he grew too much wheat! Yes, Roscoe Filburn had grown more wheat than he should have, as determined by the all-knowing, all-powerful experts at the U.S. Department of Agriculture, using their sweeping authority under the Agricultural Adjustment Act. How *dare* he become a more successful farmer than the government allowed?

Mr. Filburn challenged the fines levied against him by noting that the wheat in question (the wheat that he had produced in excess of his assigned quota), was consumed entirely on his farm, where he used it to feed his family and livestock, and kept what was left to use as seed for the next season. The wheat he grew in violation of federal law, having never left his farm, had never entered interstate commerce. This, Filburn argued, placed that wheat beyond Congress's power (which Congress had delegated to the Secretary of Agriculture) under the Commerce Clause. The Supreme Court rejected that argument, relying on its prior ruling in *Jones & Laughlin Steel*, and reasoning that even the wheat that Mr. Filburn produced and consumed entirely on his farm could "have a substantial effect" on the interstate wheat market, placing it within Congress's Commerce Clause authority.

Predictably, the Court's rulings in *Jones & Laughlin Steel* and *Wickard* have all but eliminated meaningful limits on

Congress's authority under the Commerce Clause. In fact, in the eighty-five-year period since April 12, 1937, the Supreme Court has in only three instances identified a federal statute as having been enacted outside Congress's Commerce Clause authority. Two of those laws—one of which made it a federal crime to possess a gun within a school zone, *United States v. Lopez*, while the other created a federal civil remedy available to the victims of gender-motivated violence, *United States v. Morrison*—Congress basically got caught being sloppy, managing to color outside of the (exceptionally broad) boundaries outlined by the Supreme Court. In the third instance, *National Federation of Independent Business v. Sebelius* in 2012, the Court concluded that Congress lacked authority under the Commerce Clause to order every American, under threat of significant fines, to purchase health insurance as directed by the Patient Protection and Affordable Care Act of 2010 ("Obamacare"), but then essentially rewrote that law in order to uphold it as a valid exercise of Congress's power to impose taxes.

It is thus apparent that what happed in 1937 opened the floodgates, and it made almost any activity—so long as Congress properly articulates the connection to interstate commerce properly and utters the right words in the right sequence—fair game for federal legislation. This kind of outcome is difficult to reconcile with the foundational constitutional principle of federalism. If the collective powers of Congress—or for that matter, if *any* power of Congress, including the Commerce Clause—can be given an essentially open-ended interpretation, then it is no longer true that the powers of Congress are "few and defined," while those reserved to the States are "numerous and indefinite."

But indirectly, the Supreme Court's open-ended interpretation of the Commerce Clause also affected the "horizontal" separation of powers. Once the Supreme Court handed Congress the ability to effectively be the judge of its own power (which is not unlike handing a bag of cocaine, a bottle of liquor, and car keys to a group of delinquent teenagers and hoping they'll make the right choice), Congress decided to give itself *much* more power. And in the decades that followed, Congress would panic over that. They had the power to regulate essentially anything and everything, but they didn't want the complexity and accountability that comes with it, so they started delegating their legislative authority to personnel within the executive branch (whether to the president personally, to a cabinet-level official, or to a lower-level bureaucrat who may or may not even stand accountable to the president)!

The legal framework at issue in *Wickard* v. *Filburn* actually illustrates this phenomenon perfectly. Congress and FDR wanted to control agricultural production nationwide, but didn't have the expertise, patience, or confidence necessary to tell every farmer in America how much of a particular product they could grow in a particular year. But they really, really wanted *someone* to do it, so they gave that job—and that authority—to the experts at the Department of Agriculture. That's a problem because, by doing that, they turned the

Secretary of Agriculture into a super-legislator. And the Constitution wisely entrusts the task of making federal law only to Congress—not because its members are wise, but because the power they wield is unusually dangerous, and should therefore be given only to the branch of government that is most accountable to the people at the most regular intervals. The American people have the chance to replace every member of the House and one-third of the Senate every two years. The opportunity to replace a president arises less frequently, and they *never* get that chance with respect to bureaucrats or even members of the president's cabinet. That's a problem—not just from a constitutional perspective, but also from the perspective that the kind of sweeping, discretionary power wielded by many unelected, unaccountable federal officials is utterly at odds with the concept of government of the people, by the people, and for the people. That has historically been associated with tyranny.

You might imagine that this approach was unique to (or more common during) the New Deal era. It was not. If anything, it's become far more common since then. As a result, it is now somewhat common for Congress to pass as "legislation" broad general statements accompanied by an even broader delegation of authority.

Imagine, for example, a law providing that "every workplace in America shall be safe." That sounds great, right? But because it's difficult to get lawmakers to agree on the essential elements of workplace safety, and because workplace safety can differ significantly from one profession to another and even one state to another, Congress decides to put all of the pesky line-drawing in the hands of experts, who can take the heat when unpopular decisions anger those most adversely affected by the law. To that end, Congress enacts language as part of the same bill providing in essence "we hereby delegate to the Occupational Safety and Health Administration the power to make and enforce laws to make every workplace in America safe." What, then, happens when OSHA imposes regulations requiring employers nationwide to fire unvaccinated workers, coercing them into compliance by threatening crippling fines on anyone who fails to comply? Predictably, members of Congress—even those who voted to enact legislation legitimizing this unique form of bureaucratic tyranny—will deny any accountability for such bureaucratic abuse. Much of the time, they won't even support, much less introduce legislation to clip the wings of a federal agency that has badly abused its power. Most of the time, however, they will thump their chests as they issue press releases and write harshly worded letters, complaining on behalf of their aggrieved constituents, as if they themselves had not empowered that agency.

In this fashion, the erosion of federalism—enabled by the Supreme Court's ruling in *NLRB* v. *Jones & Laughlin Steel*, has steadily led to the destruction of separation of powers. It is unclear to me whether anyone at any point was acting consciously with that mind-set, but that is what happened, and it has had disastrous consequences for the United States.

In the years to come, Justice Owen Roberts, a man who had never liked to admit wrongdoing in any way, would insist that his switch had nothing to do with politics. In fact, in papers provided to Felix Frankfurter on the condition that they be published only after he had died, Roberts argued (rather unconvincingly, in my view) that he had not switched positions at all when he ruled in *West Coast Hotel Co.* v. *Parrish*. His reasoning on the matter, he wrote, hadn't changed at all.

Even at the time, very few people believed him. But luckily for Roberts, his "switch in time" did not remain the story for very long. On May 18, 1937, Justice Willis Van Devanter, the most prominent of the Four Horsemen, announced that he would resign. Obviously, he knew that because of Justice Roberts's actions, the Court would be safe from Roosevelt's meddling. It was a stunning announcement in a season that was already full of them.

For Roosevelt, it must have felt like another victory. Although Justice Van Devanter had not been as prominent and vocal a critic of Roosevelt as his mean and often intolerant colleague James McReynolds—who once said that he would "never resign as long as that crippled son-of-a-bitch [was] in the White House,"[4]—he was an enemy nonetheless, and he had made life quite difficult for the Roosevelt administration. With him gone, Roosevelt now had two reasons to abandon his Court-packing plan for good.

But Roosevelt would not relent. No one at the time was quite sure why, and historians still argue over the precise reasons for his unwillingness to give up the fight. One potential reason is rooted in simple politics, the thing you're never supposed to allow within screaming distance of the Supreme Court. Roosevelt, as some of his aides remembered with dismay, had promised a Supreme Court seat to Senator Joe Robinson as long as the senator would defend his court-packing plan in Congress. For so many arduous months, Senator Robinson had been holding up his end of the bargain, giving impassioned (if ineffective) speeches about the need to liberalize the Court and bring it into line with modern sensibilities.

Now that there was a Supreme Court seat to offer, Roosevelt was in trouble. While Robinson had been happy to defend the Roosevelt administration on the floor of the Senate—there was something in it for him, after all—he was, like so many lawyers, a jurist at heart. The Constitution mattered to him more than the approval of the White House. Roosevelt knew that once Senator Robinson became Justice Robinson—and given how clearly he had made the promise, this outcome seemed nearly impossible to avoid, at least without some kind of political disaster—the man would issue rulings based on his understanding of the law rather than politics, which would put Roosevelt right back where he'd started: with an unbalanced Court that was unwilling to let him do whatever he pleased.

So he kept up the fight in Congress, and the results were disastrous. On June 14, the Senate Judiciary Committee voted 10 to 8 to prevent the bill from going to a floor vote. Then, in a strange twist of fate that occurred just a few days later, Senator

Joe Robinson was found dead in his apartment. He had apparently died of a heart attack, having been discovered by the maid lying next to his bed. Some of his associates, according to rumors, said that it had been the fight over the Court that killed him.

It wasn't long afterward that the bill died for good.

So what, in the end, actually saved the United States from a century of unquestioned rule by a reactionary Court of fifteen? In one sense, it was the American people, who were so opposed to Roosevelt's plot from the beginning that it became nearly impossible for him to go on. It was also the United States Senate, particularly the Judiciary Committee, whose members (most of them, anyway) refused to give the bill enough momentum to pass.

One could credibly argue that what stopped FDR's plan to pack the Court was a single man who decided to change his vote in a single case—and this part should scare you—for reasons that were by all accounts entirely political, not judicial. But I can't bring myself to praise Justice Owen Roberts's decision. If in fact Roberts changed his vote to achieve *any* political outcome, then doing so was a shameful betrayal of his judicial oath, regardless of whatever good he may have been trying to accomplish. His job was to decide cases according to the law and the facts of each case—not to achieve whatever he regarded as in the best interests of the Court and its members.

In all fairness, we don't know what would have happened if Justice Owen Roberts had reached different conclusions during those pivotal deliberations in the spring of 1937. It's easy to speculate that, had Justice Roberts stuck with the Four Horsemen, the Supreme Court as we know it would no longer exist. Maybe it would exist, but it would be several times its current size. Roosevelt's initial round of packing could have kicked off a ratchet effect, with Republicans adding more justices the next time they gained power. The Court would thereby experience an increase in its total membership with every partisan shift in Congress, rarely if ever to see a corresponding decrease (given that, once someone is confirmed to a seat on the Supreme Court, that seat cannot be eliminated unless or until the person holding it dies, retires, or is removed from office).

But we don't know any of that, and we never will. It's entirely possible that Roberts could have stayed the course, and FDR's plan to pack the Court still would have failed because of the death of Senator Robinson. Or because of Justice Van Devanter's retirement. Or because the plan was never popular with the American people, or even in Congress. We don't know, and we never will. But we do know what happened as a result of what Roberts did, and it isn't pretty—even though many of us have been taught to believe otherwise.

Writing in their report on the bill a few days before it finally died, the Senate Judiciary Committee—a committee on which I proudly serve today—wrote a short report on FDR's attempt to pack the Court. It remains one of the most important documents that the committee has ever produced. In it, the senators concluded that the bill amounted to "an invasion of judicial power such as has never before been attempted" and a "dangerous abandonment of constitutional principle."

In conclusion, they wrote that the bill "should be so emphatically rejected that its parallel will never again be presented to the free representatives of the free people of America."[5]

Looking back, you might think that FDR's bill *was* rejected that soundly, and that society remains safe from another similar attack. But that is not the case. Had it not been for a few strange accidents, it might very well have survived the attacks, just like FDR's New Deal legislation did.

And as we've seen in the past few years, the effort to pack the Supreme Court for political purposes is not, in fact, dead at all.

CHAPTER SIX

An Independent Court

B Y THE TIME I BEGAN VISITING THE SUPREME COURT in the early 1980s, there had been nine justices for well over a century. That number, which had been fought over for so long in the early years of our republic, had finally come to seem like an inevitable fact of life. In my mind, the Supreme Court had nine justices in the same way that the nation had one president, or the Utah Jazz had five players on their starting lineup. Sitting in the Court, it was as if those men who designed the building had simply come across those nine high-backed leather chairs sitting in the dirt, shrugged their shoulders, and constructed this whole vast, marble temple around them.

I didn't know—and I'm sure that most Americans didn't know—just how vulnerable the Court still remained after the events of 1937. After all, the Constitution still said nothing about the number of justices who should serve on the bench. Congress still had the power to add justices or take them away with legislation. So far, all attempts to change that had failed.

In January of 1953, for instance, a senator from Maryland named John Marshall Butler proposed a new constitutional amendment that would have, among other things, permanently fixed the number of Supreme Court justices at nine. It also would have set 75 as the mandatory retirement age for justices, ensured that justices could not run for public office once they left the Court, and also given them more of a say in the cases they would decide. Senator Butler had served as an infantryman in the First World War, and he'd been a lawyer during the Court-packing fights of the 1930s. He understood as well as anyone the importance of keeping the judicial branch insulated from politics.

Introducing his amendment on the floor of the Senate in late 1953, Senator Butler cast the debate in grand terms.

"My colleagues well know," he said, "that to [John] Locke's 'Wherever law ends, tyranny begins' there always should be added the truism that, wherever courts suffer an invasion of their independence, law ends."[1]

Given the events of previous decades, this argument had special relevance. In the years leading up to the Second World War, the world had watched as several fascist dictators had come to power in part by invading the independence of their court systems. Adolf Hitler had done it in Germany, and Benito Mussolini had done it in Italy. Countless Americans— including many senators and congressmen—had sent their sons to fight these very dictators, and they did not want to see the same thing happen in the United States. Senator Butler knew it.

"Long before the tragic demonstrations by recent and contemporaneous foreign dictators making a mockery of constitutional rights," he said, "Americans had learned that written compacts and charters can be no more effective as guarantors of liberty than the vitality given to them by an independent judiciary charged with the duty of construction and enforcement. While Americans will rally to the defense of the judiciary whenever it is subjected to an open assault, attention also should be devoted by us to the prevention of future attacks, especially upon new fronts."[2]

The initial speech didn't garner much attention from the press, which is understandable. As of this writing, there have been almost 12,000 proposed amendments to the Constitution, many of them originating on the floor of the Senate. Many, if not most of them, are introduced with the same life-and-death, world-historical kind of spin that Senator Butler had put on his own amendment. But our system of government makes it so incredibly difficult to amend the Constitution— and rightly so—that only the most serious proposals ever make their way through the dark sea of subcommittees and hearing rooms up to the surface where the American people can see them.

But in this case, a small subcommittee hearing on the amendment attracted the attention of several major newspapers. But it wasn't because of the contents of the amendment, or because of anything that the senators on the subcommittee had said. Rather, the press and the American people were interested because Owen Roberts, the former Supreme Court justice who had become famous for the "switch in time that saved nine," would be traveling from rural Pennsylvania, where he had lived since retiring in 1945, to Washington, DC, to give a rare public statement at the hearing.

In the ten years since he stepped down from the Supreme Court, Roberts had largely stepped away from public life, serving only a few years as the dean of the law school at the University of Pennsylvania. So far, he had given no indication that he felt guilty about changing his position in *NLRB* v. *Jones & Laughlin Steel*, thereby opening the floodgates of federal regulation of interstate commerce, and eventually leading to Congress's obsession with delegating actual lawmaking to unelected, unaccountable bureaucrats. In fact, he had said virtually nothing on the matter at all, writing only two pages that he entrusted to Felix Frankfurter on the condition that they would be published only after he died. As for the rest of his papers—the drafts of his many opinions, his correspondence with law clerks, research memos, really anything that would have given the public a window into his thinking—they were gone. Shortly after stepping down from the bench, Roberts had burned them.

This might have been for the best. By the end of his tenure on the Court, according to an account by a biographer, the relationship between Roberts and his colleagues, especially Justice Hugo Black, had deteriorated.[3] Things were so bad that in his last weeks, the other justices refused to send him the customary letter of congratulations that usually accompanies a justice's retirement. In the world of the Supreme Court, where tradition and decorum are almost a religion, this was as close to a public rebuke as the judges were likely to get. The "clash of strong wills" was reported in the press, albeit mostly relegated to gossip columns, and it stoked further public interest in exactly what had occurred during the Court-packing fights of the late 1930s.

But Justice Roberts still wasn't talking.

At the beginning of the hearing, Roberts maintained his silence, sitting quietly in his seat. Along with a small crowd in the chamber, he listened to an opening statement from Senator Butler, who noted that for the first time in a while, the Court seemed to be "surrounded by an aura of tranquility." This was true. In the aftermath of President Roosevelt's assault on the Supreme Court, the institution had gone relatively quiet. It had also continued to uphold large portions of President Roosevelt's New Deal, which is exactly what the president had intended during his Court-packing fight. Also, thanks to the unprecedented four terms that he served in office, Roosevelt had been able to nominate a record eight justices to the bench, the most since Chief Justice William Howard Taft's presidency.

Justice George Sutherland, sensing that the balance of power was shifting away from him, had resigned in 1938, about a year after the infamous "switch in time." Roosevelt replaced him with Stanley F. Reed, his liberal solicitor general. The rest of the Four Horsemen had then left the Court in fairly rapid succession, with Pierce Butler dying in 1939 and

James McReynolds stepping down in 1941. Given that Willis Van Devanter had already stepped down in mid-1937, that meant they were all gone. Finally, Roosevelt had gotten his way. Among their replacements was Felix Frankfurter, who had been vital to President Roosevelt during his fight to pack the Court. By the time World War II began, President Roosevelt had almost completely remade the Supreme Court in his own image.

During the war, Justice Owen Roberts himself had left the Court entirely for a period, serving as the head of a commission to investigate the Pearl Harbor attacks. His findings, in part, had helped pave the way for President Roosevelt's later Shameful, Xenophobic internment of Japanese Americans, something Roberts voted against as a justice.

Of course, no one was interested in that during the hearing. What they wanted from former Justice Roberts was a clear, strong denunciation of President Roosevelt's attempt to destroy the Court on which Roberts had proudly served for fifteen years. They wanted something that would make the next day's newspapers, drum up public support, and lead to the passage of an amendment that would, finally, secure a guarantee that the Court could never be packed again. They might also have wanted some admission that he had bowed to public pressure from President Roosevelt, changing his vote and permanently weakening the once-significant distinction between state and federal power.

Once again, Owen Roberts disappointed them.

During his address to the subcommittee—which he delivered rather eloquently without recourse to notes, an impressive feat for a retiree who was then pushing eighty—Roberts spent a long time making the case that justices should not run for office, and also spoke at length about a few jurisdictional issues that had arisen during a case more than fifty years earlier. Only in the middle of his address did he mention the fight to pack the Court, and even then, it was to refer to the letter that Chief Justice Hughes had written to the Senate Judiciary Committee in the midst of the ordeal.

"Now," he said a few minutes into his statement. "I do not need to refer to the Court-packing plan which was resorted to when I was a member of the Court. Apart from the tremendous strain and threat to the existing Court, of which I was fully conscious, it is obviously, if ever resorted to, a political device to influence the Court and to pack it so as to be in conformity with the views of the Executive, or the Congress, or both."[4]

This was as close as Justice Roberts would ever come to admitting that he had made the infamous "switch in time" that has long been credited (rightly or not) with saving the independence of the Supreme Court.

The next day, he was quoted in *The New York Times* in an article about the proposed amendment. "Former Supreme Court Justice Owen J. Roberts said today a 'bitter' Congress might someday 'pack' or restrict the Supreme Court," it read. "He urged the adoption of a constitutional amendment to prevent such a possibility."[5]

The article, which appeared at the very bottom of page 8 below three other notices of new constitutional amendments, did not make much of a stir. While it gained a fair amount of support, especially in the Senate, the effort did not show any sign that it would actually gain the support it needed to make it into the Constitution—a burden that, remember, the founders made difficult to meet. Shortly afterward, the proposed amendment officially died in the Senate. Owen Roberts, who appeared even less frequently in public after the hearing, died a few months later in May of 1955.

And so, it might be argued, the real last chance that we had to safeguard the Supreme Court through legislative means—meaning a constitutional amendment that could have been written, debated, and adopted while those who had lived through the clamor of FDR's Court-packing fight were still alive and working in Washington, DC—slipped away.

Future attempts would meet a similar fate.

In effect, this left an imaginary big red button, right on the wall of the Oval Office, with words that read "PUSH HERE TO PACK THE COURT" in big, bold letters. It is a "break glass in case of emergency" measure, to be sure, but it is one that remains available to any president willing to cast tradition and decency aside and take the political risk. The system, after all, is still in place. To make it work, a president (necessarily one whose party holds majorities in both houses of Congress) could use his enormous bully pulpit to cast himself as the hero of the American story, identify the existing Supreme Court as the villain, and then convince the American people that they desperately needed him to pack the Court into submission. If he succeeded on that front, a Court-packing bill might actually pass through Congress and arrive on his desk for his signature. But even if the bill didn't pass, if the president made enough headway, the entire process might scare the Court (or even a single justice) into deciding cases in a manner more to his liking.

Sadly, it was still—and it remains today—that easy. And it's not like anyone is surprised by this, either.

In the late nineteenth century, a scholar from England named James Bryce came to the United States and noticed this big red button, although he didn't refer to it as such. When he published his findings in the two-volume work titled *The American Commonwealth* in 1888, Bryce had almost nothing but praise for the American system of government. As a Scotsman, he marveled at the structure set up by our Constitution in much the same manner that Alexis de Tocqueville had a century earlier in his landmark *Democracy in America*. Speaking of Bryce's work in later years, Chief Justice William Howard Taft would claim that he "knew us better than we know ourselves, and he went about and among us and gave us the boon of his illuminating wisdom derived from the lessons of the past."[6]

Tellingly, when Bryce considers the failure of our founders to fix the number of Supreme Court justices, his prose turns dark, and he issues a dire warning to future Americans. "Suppose," he writes, a Congress and president bent on doing something which the Supreme Court deems contrary to the Constitution. They pass a statute. A case arises under it. The Court on the hearing of the case unanimously declares the statute to be null, as being beyond the powers of Congress. Congress forthwith passes and the president signs another statute more than doubling the number of justices. The president appoints to the new justiceships men who are pledged to hold the former statute constitutional. The Senate confirms the appointments. Another case raising the validity of the disputed statute is brought up to the court. The new justices outvote the old ones; the statute is held valid; the security provided for the protection of the Constitution is gone like a morning mist.[7]

At this point I'm sure I don't have to point out that this is almost exactly what happened to our judicial system in the 1930s, albeit in a slightly different form. President Roosevelt was not getting the ruling that he wanted, so he threatened to pack the Supreme Court with justices who would give him better answers—and he would have gone around Congress to do it. But it was not the Constitution that saved us. Rather, it was the actions of a few opponents in Congress, an upswelling of negative public opinion, and several unlikely accidents that stopped him from being able to follow through on his plan. But the danger survived.

Earlier in *The American Commonwealth*, Bryce refers to the lack of protection for our judiciary as "a weak point, a joint in the Court's armor through which a weapon might someday penetrate," which is perhaps a better metaphor than the big red button I used earlier.

For years, this joint in the Court's armor has been there, sitting out in the open, just waiting for a president or Congress to drive a sword right through it.

———•———

So far, nobody has driven that sword all the way through.

In fact, for decades after President Roosevelt's Court-packing plan died on the floor of the Senate, not a single president from either party has even suggested trying something like it again. In the years immediately following the debacle, most of those who lived through it—or, at the very least, studied it as recent political history—seemed to have learned their lesson. Even though the attempts to safeguard the Supreme Court always failed, there was an unspoken rule that the Supreme Court was not to be touched.

The results were remarkable. For most of the twentieth century, the Supreme Court operated with as much independence as ever, and maybe even more. The justices, sensing that they were safe from political maneuvering in either Congress or the executive branch, were free to read and interpret the law according to their own judgment, which is exactly what the framers of our Constitution intended. Most of the time, this led to unanimous or near-unanimous rulings and widespread agreement among the justices. But there were also split decisions, clashes between justices, and decisions that ruffled feathers in the executive branch and elsewhere. And yet the Court survived as an independent, coordinate branch, maintaining its legitimacy and credibility because—despite its flaws and mistakes—it is still the best tribunal of its kind anywhere on earth.

This new era of independence began, in some sense, on September 30, 1953, when President Dwight D. Eisenhower nominated Earl Warren, the former governor of California, to become the next chief justice of the Supreme Court.

At the time, the Court was without a leader, both literally and figuratively. The previous chief justice, a former representative and judge named Fred Vinson, had been found dead in his home just two weeks earlier. To his colleagues, nearly all of whom had been nominated by President Roosevelt during his unprecedented twelve years in office, Vinson's death was a surprise, although not an unwelcome one. Most of them had been cordial about his death, with the exception of one. After releasing a short statement on the matter, Felix Frankfurter— who had been nominated to the Court by Roosevelt in 1939— said that Chief Justice Vinson's death had "provided him with the first solid evidence of the existence of God."[8]

To many, Earl Warren seemed like an odd choice. He was, after all, much better known as a politician than as a lawyer, and had no professional background as a jurist or law professor. Most accounts describe Warren as not particularly charismatic, and he had never especially distinguished himself as a scholar or a writer. But he had managed to win three terms as governor of California, and he had taken conservative stances on several issues. To President Eisenhower and Herbert Brownell, Eisenhower's attorney general and de facto advisor on judicial appointments, this was important. They were facing the most liberal Court in the history of the United States, and they wanted someone who could bring things back to order.

On October 5, Warren was sworn in as chief justice, and the era of the "Warren Court" began.

For a few years, Chief Justice Warren and his associate justices ruled on cases in the manner that the founding fathers intended. They heard the facts of a given case, read the Constitution, studied the history, and applied the law with care. In 1954, for instance, the same year that Senator John Marshall Butler failed to pass his amendment to protect the Supreme Court, the justices overruled *Plessy* v. *Ferguson*, a decision that had established the evil and blatantly unconstitutional doctrine of "separate but equal"—in the landmark case *Brown* v. *Board of Education*. The ruling was unanimous.

According to the majority opinion, written by Chief Justice Warren himself, the "segregation of white and colored children in public schools has a detrimental effect upon the colored children. The impact is greater," he continued, "when it has the sanction of the law, for the policy of separating the races is usually interpreted as denoting the inferiority of the Negro group...Any language in contrary to this finding is rejected. We conclude that in the field of public education the doctrine of 'separate but equal' has no place. Separate educational facilities are inherently unequal."[9]

The Court made the right and just decision. But given the political climate at the time, many people—including some in the Congress and the executive branch—believed it was wrong, or, at the very least, the wrong way to go about doing the right thing. In the months and years after the Supreme Court's decision, billboards reading "IMPEACH EARL WARREN" began popping up all over the South. There was chaos in the streets, and horrible scenes unfolding in front of high schools that were about to be de-segregated. For a president hoping to be reelected, the chaos was difficult to take. Speaking to an aide about the decision, President Eisenhower called his appointment of Warren to the Supreme Court "the biggest damn fool mistake I ever made."[10] He also told Attorney General Brownell to refrain from nominating anyone to the Court who hadn't previously been a judge; without a record of decisions, it was impossible to tell how someone would rule.

But there was no official talk of impeaching Warren. Even politicians who wanted to reverse the Court's ruling were not making attempts to do so through any means other than those delegated to the other two branches in the United States Constitution. As angry as some of the comments from the executive branch directed toward the Supreme Court got—and in the years to come, they would get *very* angry—the subject of packing the Court did not come up again in any serious way. Once again, the Supreme Court appeared safe from the meddling of presidents and Congress. The Court was insulated from politics as it had never been before, making decisions that often went against public opinion, or at least popular opinion within the other two branches.

Inside the Court itself, however, political concerns were working their way in. This shouldn't have been surprising, given that the man at the top was himself a politician.

For the rest of Warren's term, it would become clear just how badly Eisenhower had misjudged the former governor of California. In the words of *The New York Times*, his votes over the next few years "illustrated the phenomenon of a man growing more liberal with age."[11] However, in Warren's case, "liberal" is probably not the right word. What the reporter surely meant was that during his time on the Court, Warren and his fellow justices grew much more comfortable *making* laws rather than reading and interpreting them. Throughout the 1960s, the Warren Court began developing a constitutional philosophy on the doctrine of "unenumerated rights," claiming that, just because a right wasn't protected by a particular provision in the Constitution, that didn't mean that such a right could not exist. For inspiration, they took the philosophy of a "living Constitution," believing that the words of the document changed with the evolving standards of our time.

By the time Chief Justice Warren began contemplating his retirement in 1968—the same year that his old rival, Richard Nixon, was mounting a successful campaign to win the White House—this open, interpretive approach to the Constitution was ascendant. The Supreme Court, in the view of many voters, had brought about a great deal of social change, which some welcomed. But they also knew that the Warren Court had—in contrast to what it had done in *Brown* v. *Board of Education*, where it stood on solid constitutional ground—at times relied on shaky legal reasoning to reach a desired result. In reinterpreting the Constitution to make it conform to the justices' own, subjective, progressive, and ever-changing worldviews, the Supreme Court was beginning in some cases to act more like a legislative body than a judicial one. Legislative bodies establish policy and must think prospectively, deciding *what the law should* and *will be* moving forward. Judicial bodies, by contrast, look back in time to assess *what the law was* at a particular moment in time. While not everyone agrees as to which cases were decided correctly and which were not, it's difficult to dispute that it's a dangerous thing for the Court to venture far beyond the law and Constitution while purporting to interpret the relevant text (providing an objective assessment of *what the law was* at the moment in question) to decide a particular case.

The voters, it seemed, were ready to try something else.

On the campaign trail, Richard Nixon had given several speeches regarding the sort of justices he would nominate to the Supreme Court if he were to become president. In many ways, his campaign represents the first time that the concept of "textualism"—*i.e.*, the idea that the job of the jurist is to discern the public meaning of the relevant law, as of the moment of its enactment—made its way into the public consciousness as a judicial philosophy. The approach known as "originalism" involves essentially the same effort, but specifically used to interpret the Constitution.

Speaking a few weeks before the election about the type of person he would nominate if he won the White House, Nixon said: "They would see their duty as interpreting the law rather than making the law. They would see themselves as caretakers of the Constitution and servants of the people, not super-legislators with a free hand to impose their political and social viewpoints upon the American system and the American people."[12]

By this point, it was public knowledge that four months earlier, Earl Warren had submitted his resignation letter to President Lyndon Johnson. Knowing that it was possible that Nixon would win the White House and appoint what he called "strict constructionist" justices to the high Court, Warren had taken special care to say that he would retire *only* when his successor was confirmed. President Johnson quickly named a replacement—back then, Senate Democrats apparently didn't object trying to "rush through" a nominee in the months immediately preceding a presidential election when the president's party controlled a majority of the votes in the Senate, as Democrats did at the time. Notwithstanding that majority, the nomination failed in the Senate.

Still, Warren agreed to adhere to the terms of his resignation letter and wait for the next president to name his successor before stepping down. Of course, he was hoping at the time that the next president would be Hubert Humphrey, a liberal who had endorsed Chief Justice Warren's sometimes-unusual approach to the Constitution, not Richard Nixon, whom he intensely disliked.

Of course, things didn't go that way.

When Richard Nixon did win the election, Warren agreed to remain on the bench until June, at which point Nixon nominated Warren E. Burger to replace him. A Republican who had served many years as a judge appointed by President Eisenhower, Burger had often described himself as a "strict constructionist"—a term that has long been used (incorrectly in my view, but quite consistently) as a synonym for "textualist." In other words, Burger presented himself as exactly the type of jurist Nixon had promised to nominate to the Court during his campaign. But Nixon, like so many presidents before him, quickly learned that an appointment to the Supreme Court is no guarantee of loyalty. In the years to come, Warren Burger and the other justices nominated by Richard Nixon would issue several rulings that caused deep frustration within the Nixon administration, even playing a major role in the demise of his presidency.

In 1971, for instance, the Supreme Court heard a case involving *The New York Times*, *The Washington Post*, and the federal government. A few years earlier, Secretary of Defense Robert McNamara had commissioned a report on the progress of America's war in Vietnam. With American casualties mounting, the public was beginning to lose hope. When Daniel Ellsberg, a special assistant at the Pentagon, read the report, he was horrified. The "Pentagon Papers," as they would come to be known, revealed not only that the war in Vietnam was a failure, but that the White House had lied about it.

Throughout the winter of 1971, Ellsberg passed photocopies of the report to Neil Sheehan at *The New York Times*, and the paper began publishing excerpts in June of that year. Initially, President Nixon planned to do nothing about it, given that *he* wasn't the one who had done all the lying; that had been his political rivals, John F. Kennedy and Lyndon Johnson. But on the advice of Henry Kissinger, Nixon took action and attempted to block publication by the *Times* and *The Washington Post*, which also had excerpts. This was a classic, and quite difficult, case of what limits should be placed on the First Amendment, and the details of it are fascinating to anyone interested in how to interpret the United States Constitution.

The case, *New York Times Co.* v. *United States*, went before the Supreme Court on June 26, 1971, and it was decided four days later, on June 30. Despite a compelling argument by the government that publishing the documents posed a threat to national security, the Court ruled 6–3 that the newspapers did indeed have the right to publish the material under the First Amendment. This case is considered among the most important precedents in First Amendment jurisprudence to this day. And it might have come out differently if the Supreme Court had not established itself as an independent branch that was free from political concerns.

President Nixon, of course, was not happy with the result. But he didn't attempt to pack the Court as President Roosevelt had. Instead, he played the game according to the rules, nominating people to fill vacancies only as they arose. This he did a total of four times, first with Chief Justice Burger, and then with Associate Justices Harry Blackmun, Lewis Powell, and William Rehnquist. In Nixon's view, all three of them— like Chief Justice Burger—had through their prior rulings exhibited an unwillingness to "legislate from the bench." This, he assumed, would give him more favorable rulings in the future.

Again, he was wrong. Three years later, in July of 1974, President Nixon stood accused of orchestrating a break-in at the Democratic National Committee headquarters during the presidential campaign of 1972, a scandal that would come to be known as "Watergate." The president's involvement in this break-in, as well as his attempts to cover it up, were believed to be documented on a series of taped conversations that occurred in the Oval Office, and Nixon's representatives had attempted several times to block the release of these tapes in Court, failing every time. Eventually, the case reached the Supreme Court, and the public wondered whether the Court might rule in Nixon's favor, given that he had effectively given four of them their jobs.

But it didn't happen. After then-Associate Justice William

Rehnquist (who had served as Nixon's deputy attorney general) recused himself, the Supreme Court delivered a unanimous opinion that effectively ordered President Nixon to turn over the tapes. Nixon resigned sixteen days after the ruling was handed down.

If nothing else, this case is a reminder that those who serve on the Supreme Court—who typically hear only those cases that have been the most contentious, and in which lower courts have been unable to agree as to the correct answer to the same question of federal law—often find themselves in complete agreement. It also illustrates how even during some of the most heated political debates of the twentieth century, the Court did not give in to political influence from either the Right or the Left. Even as the media attempted to throw particular justices or opinions into the same "liberal/conservative," "left/right," "Democratic/Republican" baskets that they used for the other branches, the Court went about its work without any discernible hesitation or preoccupation with its image. Any divide between the Court's members, they knew, had nothing to do with so-called liberal or conservative opinions about particular policies. Rather, it was a disagreement about the proper way to interpret the law and Constitution, a matter on which legal minds have disagreed for decades.

For the next few decades, the Court's radical independence continued unabated, and it did so despite an unusually partisan political environment. In its 1992 ruling in *Planned Parenthood* v. *Casey*, the Court upheld the most substantial portions of *Roe* v. *Wade.* That outcome upset many conservatives, who had hoped that case would turn out differently.

In 2000, the Court decided *Bush* v. *Gore,* helping to resolve one of the closest and most contentious presidential elections in American history. This upset many liberals, who had hoped that the case would turn out differently. In 2012, the Court decided *NFIB* v. *Sebelius,* 567 U.S. 519 (2012), upholding Obamacare against two separate constitutional challenges (essentially rewriting the law—in two meaningful respects—in order to uphold it). This upset many conservatives, who had hoped that the case would turn out differently. This list could go on and on, but you get the point.

Through all this, the Court *still* managed to come out relatively unscathed, preserving its reputation of fidelity to the law above all else. By sticking close to the Constitution—or, at least, by keeping the battle between textualism and the "living Constitution" relatively confined to its chambers, and keeping the bitter left-right politics of the other two branches out of its deliberations—the Supreme Court managed to act in precisely the manner directed by the Constitution: as a politically neutral adjudicative body that, when allowed to do its job, could safeguard the rights of the American people.

There were congressional hearings on the subject, to be sure, and the hatred for the Court—especially during the Warren era—was palpable. But the notion that anyone would try to pack the Court again never surfaced. Even during some of the most heated battles in our nation's history—over segregation, civil rights, and abortion—the mere hint of Court packing would have been considered a gross violation of norms, a "nuclear" option that you'd only consider if you were willing to burn the whole country down to get what you want.

In other words: it was something that only the Democratic Party of the early 2020s would even consider.

CHAPTER SEVEN

From "Bonehead" to Mainstream

THERE IS NO SHORTAGE OF BAD IDEAS IN AMERICAN politics. They're everywhere. These days, given the current occupant of the White House, you need only look at your Twitter feed or open a newspaper to see a few in action. In fact, since January 20, 2021, we've seen more policies than ever move from the radical fringes of the Left into the spotlight. From incremental steps toward socialism and the Green New Deal to government surveillance, extreme tax hikes, and threats to fire every American worker who doesn't comply with the presidential medical orthodoxy of the day, the Biden administration has yanked our national policy conversations in a far leftward direction. In most cases, it's relatively difficult to pinpoint the exact moment when these ideas first entered the mainstream, moving from the dark basements of think tanks and liberal interest groups into the living rooms of Americans everywhere.

With Court packing, however, it's not difficult at all.

The idea got "mainstreamed" on the evening of September 29, 2020, when Joe Biden met President Donald Trump on the debate stage for the first time. I'm sure you remember. In hindsight, this initial debate wasn't a stellar performance by either candidate. If you watch the clips on YouTube, you'll find that the whole thing quickly devolves into a mess of hurled insults, half-finished sentences, and several attempts by Chris Wallace, who moderated, to keep his head above water. But the passion on both sides was understandable.

The stakes, after all, were extremely high.

Less than two weeks earlier, Justice Ruth Bader Ginsburg, a legend of the Supreme Court, had died suddenly of cancer. Despite the rumors that had been circulating for years about her failing health, Justice Ginsburg's death still came as something of a shock to those in Washington, especially to those of us who had been following her remarkable career for decades.

As someone who fervently believed in the "living constitution" approach to jurisprudence, Justice Ginsburg had never been my model of how a justice should interpret the law. As a textualist myself, it's safe to say that she and I didn't always agree on matters of constitutional interpretation. But her dedication to her job on the Court was inspiring, and her close friendship with her colleagues—most notably Justice Antonin Scalia, who often referred to Ginsburg as his "best buddy" on the Court despite disagreeing with her vehemently on important issues—was a model of civility in a world where it seemed to be disappearing. In the words of Justice Scalia, who sometimes appeared in public with Justice Ginsburg for lively back-and-forth chats about the Supreme Court, "What's not to like? Except her views of the *law*, of course."[1]

I got a taste of this during the year that I served as a law clerk for Justice Samuel Alito, for whom I had previously clerked when he served on the U.S. Court of Appeals for the Third Circuit. This was during the Court's 2006 term, when the ideological conflict between textualists and proponents of the living Constitution theory was in full swing, at least as far as the media was concerned. But that ill will never spilled into the Supreme Court.

I interacted frequently with law clerks from different chambers—liberals and conservatives alike. My three co-clerks and I were fortunate enough to have lunch with each justice at one point or another, and we were even invited to Justice Ginsburg's office for tea. Her husband had made a delightful cake for the occasion, during which we discussed a wide range of topics, legal and otherwise. One of many things that I remember about that day was that she provided herbal tea for my enjoyment (apparently she knew that, as a member of The Church of Jesus Christ of Latter-day Saints, I can drink herbal tea, but not the non-herbal variety). And even when one of my colleagues inadvertently tipped over her teapot (doing no permanent damage, but spilling its contents onto the well-set table in her office), she could not have been more gracious—just as she was in every interaction I have ever had with her.

What some people don't understand is that Americans—even Supreme Court justices—who argue with one another can usually do so without personal antipathy as long as they do it in good faith. To this day, some of my fondest memories during my time working at the Supreme Court are of hours I spent discussing pending cases with my fellow law clerks—some conservative, others liberal—while trying to figure out how best to advise our respective bosses on each case. Some of the cases we discussed were well-known, politically charged, and inherently contentious. Most were really technical, not terribly newsworthy, and of consequence to relatively few people. But regardless of the case, I found all of our conversations to be respectful.

I've tried to carry all that I learned working for Justice Alito and put it to good use, both as a lawyer and as a member of the Senate. Many of Justice Ginsburg's law clerks have likewise taken what they learned working for her and put it to good use, both in law and in politics. I tend to believe that they, like me, remain convinced that politics and the Court shouldn't mix (or at least that they should mix no more than they are required to mix by virtue of the nomination and confirmation process established by the Constitution).

Shortly after Justice Ginsburg's death, speculation arose as to who might fill the vacancy created by her passing. On September 26, 2020, President Trump followed through on his commitment to nominate a committed textualist to that position—Judge Amy Coney Barrett, who was then serving on the U.S. Court of Appeals for the Seventh Circuit and who had previously worked as a law professor, lawyer, and law clerk to Justice Antonin Scalia.

I was proud to attend her nomination ceremony in the Rose Garden and watch President Trump list off her many accomplishments. From there, I could almost hear the anguished cries from Democrats. There was good reason for them.

In all her years in the law, Amy Coney Barrett had managed never to stray from her legal principles. She had always operated according to what the law said, not what the ever-shifting standards of public opinion indicated that it *should* mean. For liberals, this must have been terrifying. For years, they had built precedents based on decisions that had come out of the "living Constitution" approach, and they were hoping to keep building for years to come. They were expecting decisions on several important issues. If these cases came before a Court that was composed primarily of textualists like Amy Coney Barrett, Brett Kavanaugh, Neil Gorsuch, Sam Alito, and Clarence Thomas, however, victory for them might not be so assured.

Again, this was not a matter of President Trump appointing a so-called "conservative" justice to the Supreme Court. As we've already covered, that's not really how it works at the Supreme Court. Rather, there are justices who believe that the words of the Constitution mean what they meant at the time that they were drafted and ratified—a view that was predominant for most of our nation's history, by the way—and there are those who believe that these words can be taken, molded, and imbued with new meaning according to the political climate of the time. Reasonable people can disagree about which approach is correct, and presidents of either party can appoint justices who have particular feelings one way or the other. But that doesn't mean that we should judge potential Supreme Court nominees based on what they feel about particular policies—a standard, by the way, that was reiterated by Ruth Bader Ginsburg herself during her own Senate nomination hearings.

So, by the time Biden reached the debate stage to face off with Donald Trump for the first time, the battle lines had already been drawn. If President Trump went through with his nomination of Amy Coney Barrett and she was confirmed in the Senate, they would have to resort to desperate measures.

But no one knew whether Biden would support it publicly—or whether he would once again denounce it, as he had so many times throughout his long career.

I didn't know either. I had heard whispers during the primaries that Democrats were going to think seriously about packing the Court; I had even heard about detailed proposals from a few of the candidates, though I didn't bother to read them. The idea seemed too far-fetched to be real. I believed that only a person who had obviously lost touch with reality would even contemplate bringing such a measure back into the public conversation. Even the most basic understanding of

American history would lead you to the conclusion that this is one of those very, *very* bad ideas that died long ago and should remain dead forever.

Finally, after fourteen minutes of bitter back-and-forth squabbling, the question came.

"There has been talk," said Chris Wallace during a rare moment of silence, "about ending the filibuster or packing the Court, adding to the nine justices there. You call this a distraction by the president, but in fact, it wasn't brought up by the president; it was brought up by some of your Democratic colleagues in the Congress. So my question to you is: you have refused in the past to talk about it. Are you willing to tell the American people tonight whether or not you will support either ending the filibuster or packing the court?"

Biden, displaying an uncharacteristic facility with words, shot back a quick nonanswer (obviously he had rehearsed and been encouraged to repeat verbatim when given the opportunity): "Whatever position I take on that, that'll become the issue. The issue is, the American people should speak."

He turned to the camera and continued, shaking one hand aloft as he seemed to lose the thread.

"You should go out and vote. You're in…voting now. Vote and let your senators know how strongly you feel."

At this point, President Trump, likely speaking for millions of viewers watching at home, pressed Biden on the issue when Chris Wallace wouldn't.

"Are you going to pack the Court?

"Why won't you answer the question?

"You don't want to answer that?"

Finally, Biden gave up on trying to justify his position, or lack thereof, and shouted: "Will you *shut up*, man?"

And that, for the moment, was that. Chris Wallace moved on to other, less pressing areas, but the damage was done. For the next week, the words "Court packing" seemed to be everywhere. Liberal websites like *Vox* wrote explainers about the term, casting FDR's first shot in a relatively favorable light. "To many leftists and Left-liberals," they wrote, "such drastic action is needed if any progressive legislation in the future is to survive—and if precedents on abortion rights and LGBTQ equality are to avoid reversal."[2]

To liberals, who had already grown used to viewing Biden as the second coming of FDR, this was all the license they needed to begin supporting the idea.

Everyone seemed to know what was going on. After all, Joe Biden hadn't been afraid to denounce some of the other wacky ideas that members of his party had put forward. He didn't have a problem, for instance, saying that the Green New Deal was a bad idea, or that he wasn't in favor of immediate tax hikes.

His dodge on the Court-packing answer meant two things: first, that he definitely had plans to add new, liberal justices to the Supreme Court—or, at the very least, a team of eager, radical liberals to do it for him; and second, that he was well aware of how politically toxic that action was.

But his refusal to answer the question was not an isolated incident. For the rest of the campaign, whenever he allowed the press pool to ask him questions, the Court-packing threat would eventually come up. But he continued to dodge.

Finally, after a few rounds of questioning, he admitted the truth: "[Voters will] know my opinion on Court packing when the election is over. It's a great question, and I don't blame you for asking it, but you know the moment I answer that question, the headline in every one of your papers will be about that."[3]

Much like House Speaker Nancy Pelosi, who once claimed that she needed to pass a bill to find out what was in it, Biden was asking us to wait.

———◆———

Of course, we didn't have to.

Anyone who watched Joe Biden dodge that question could find out exactly what the man's position on Court packing was—or, rather, what it *had* been for the fifty or so years leading up to that moment. All you need is an internet connection to find the now-famous video of then-Senator Biden discussing the concept during a hearing in July 1983. At that time, Joe Biden was a junior senator. In later years, he would go on to become the chairman of the judiciary committee. But even he knew at the time that FDR's attempt to bend the judiciary to his will had been a bad idea.

"President Roosevelt," he said in 1983, "clearly had the right to send to the United States Senate and the United States Congress a proposal to pack the court. It was totally within his right to do that. He violated no law. He was legalistically, absolutely correct. But it was a bonehead idea. It was a terrible, terrible mistake to make. And it put in question, for an entire decade, the independence of the most significant body—including the Congress in my view—the most significant body in this country, the Supreme Court of the United States of America."[4]

In the early 1980s, this wasn't a controversial opinion. In fact, Biden's statement was in line with views held by, well, essentially everyone in America. Even the most liberal law professors believed that Court packing had been, at best, a risky distraction from FDR's goals—something that had hurt him more than it had helped. Writing in a book called *God Save This Honorable Court*, which was supposed to convince readers that we needed more liberal judges on the bench, Harvard professor Laurence Tribe said that it had been FDR's "nomination power, and not the Court-packing plan, that did the job" of remaking the Court in his image.[5] At least Tribe was consistent—he remains a strident voice on the Left in favor of Court packing to this day.

In the years between FDR's attempt to pack the Court and the present day, this has been one of the rare issues on which the Right and the Left are in general agreement. They knew, as Joe Biden would say during a campaign stop, that once you open that door, it's very hard to close it again. "I would not get into court packing," he said during the event. "We add three justices. Next time around, we lose control, and they add three justices. We begin to lose any credibility the court has at all."[6]

For most people, "Court packing" was a taboo word, the way "communism" and "socialism" used to be. These terms sat on the very fringes of our public discourse, only really discussed by people who had no say in our elections. But much like communism or socialism, those words began to be rehabilitated over time. The more people heard them, the more they were okay with hearing them. By the time people seriously began putting the idea forth during the presidency of Donald Trump, certain influential people on the Left began to believe that Court packing was a serious way to deal with rulings they didn't like.

But the ideas were far from mainstream. As late as 2018, even reliably leftist thinkers wouldn't get behind it. Writing in *The New York Times* that year, for instance, the liberal historian Julian E. Zelizer, who cowrote a book with *1619 Project* contributor Kevin Kruse, warned that Court packing was "a terrible idea." The op-ed begins with a vivid description of President Roosevelt's efforts to pack the Court, much like the one I've given here, and the horrible political consequences that resulted for Roosevelt. (The proposal, Zelizer argues, led indirectly to a reactionary conservative Congress that gave Roosevelt more trouble than even the Supreme Court had.)

"If Democrats place their bets on Court-packing once again, the political backlash would probably be even more severe," he writes. "If liberals want to change the direction of the courts, they should do more to replicate the kind of long-term projects their opponents have undertaken since the 1980s to nurture judicial talent and create a deep pool for future appointments. Liberals need to do better at using congressional procedure and handling open hearings to diminish political support for conservative nominees—and obviously they need to win elections, starting in November."[7]

In the years to come, there would be so many op-eds of a similar nature that listing them here would consume almost all the pages I've got left. But it wasn't only historians. In the months leading up to the 2020 campaign season, it was hard to find a liberal icon who wasn't ready to offer a dire warning about Court packing. During an interview with NPR in 2019, Justice Ruth Bader Ginsburg herself said that she didn't feel it was the right thing to do.

"I have heard that there are some people on the Democratic side who would like to increase the number of judges," she said. "I think that was a bad idea when Franklin Delano Roosevelt tried to pack the Court."[8]

By that time, the "people on the Democratic side" she was referring to were household names, at least to people who vote in Democratic primaries. In March of 2019, Beto O'Rourke, a candidate best known for mounting a doomed campaign against my friend Ted Cruz, came out with a detailed plan for how to revamp the Court. Around the same time, Pete Butt-igieg, who would end up serving in Biden's cabinet, did the same thing. This was enough to get major media institutions writing about the idea, and that, in turn, was enough to make sure that there was at least one question about it during the first primary debate.

Back then, Biden had no trouble telling the world what his position was.

"No," he said from the debate stage. "I'm not prepared to go on and try to pack the Court, because we'll live to rue that day."

But that was before anyone believed that Biden could really become the nominee. Back then, most people assumed that it would either be Bernie Sanders or Amy Klobuchar—two Senate colleagues I've worked with and genuinely like, despite many policy disagreements. Or maybe the nod would go to one of the many lesser-known, young Democrats who had gotten into the race largely to push wacky ideas like Court packing. When Biden prevailed, I can only imagine he had armies of consultants lined up to tell him that if he had any hope of winning this election, he was going to have to embrace some of those crazy ideas that his party had come up with over the past few years. If he didn't, there was a very good chance that he wasn't going to be able to pull enough voters together to win a majority.

So he did. But he didn't say so.

Instead, he gave vague signals about them, refusing to

answer questions about Court packing in public and telling the country that they would have to wait until he was elected to see what he thought.

———

During his first few weeks in office, President Biden said very little about Court packing. He did not, as one might have expected, stage some kind of big reveal with balloons and a marching band to reveal his true thoughts on the matter. Instead, he pushed it to the side for a few months, allowing the most radical members of his party to bring up the idea for him.

But in early April, likely sensing that he could not avoid the issue for much longer, President Biden announced that he would be forming a commission to "provide an analysis of the principal arguments in the contemporary public debate for and against Supreme Court reform, including an appraisal of the merits and legality of particular reform proposals."[9] At first glance, the commission appeared to be a bipartisan coalition of conservative and liberal legal scholars from all over the country—people who would take a serious look at the evidence for and against Court packing and make a recommendation to the president. There were even rumors that President Biden had set it up this way because he wanted to *avoid* bowing to the radicals in his party and enacting Court packing. An article in *USA Today* noted, correctly, that "Biden has sent repeated signals that he has little interest in spending political capital on increasing the number of justices in the Supreme Court," and called the creation of the commission "an effort to keep that idea at arm's length."[10]

But if we learned anything during the election, it's that President Biden is no longer in charge of his own politics. The radical leftists in his party are.

A few days later, Democrats in Congress, led primarily by Congressman Jerrold Nadler of New York, Senator Ed Markey of Massachusetts, and Congressman Hank Johnson of Georgia, introduced a bill that would expand the Supreme Court from nine justices to thirteen, with twelve associate justices and one chief justice. Standing in front of the steps of the Supreme Court, they gave a press conference to a small audience of reporters, articulating the reasons for the drastic step they were taking. The cardboard sign at the front of the podium read "EXPAND THE COURT" in big white letters.

"We are here today because the United States Supreme Court is broken," Senator Markey said. "It is out of balance and it needs to be fixed...Republicans have purposely warped and weaponized the highest court of the land for their own partisan gain. Republicans seem to think that equal justice means justice for their purposes, their values, their causes. That is not equal justice. That is not the sacred duty of the Supreme Court."[11]

I consider everything in that speech utter nonsense—ironically an extension of the same tactics that some progressive activists have been using for years to sow doubt and discord about the Supreme Court. These lines might as well have been prewritten by the same activist groups that had been grading these lawmakers on their willingness to confirm Trump judges, lobbying them constantly and donating large sums of money to their campaigns in order to make sure the Supreme Court was packed in the first two years of Biden's presidency.

At the time, Nancy Pelosi said that she had no plans to bring the bill to the floor. Senator Chuck Schumer also said that he would wait and see what happened. Just about every moderate Democrat in the senate who cared to comment on the matter said something similar. Senator Dick Durbin, for instance, said that he would hold off on a decision until he saw results from President Biden's commission.

But behind the scenes, the activists were still working.

"Progressives understand we cannot afford to wait six months for an academic study to tell us what we already know: the Supreme Court is broken and in need of reform," said Brian Fallon, a former Hillary Clinton aide who formed the group Demand Justice shortly after the 2016 election for the sole purpose of influencing our judicial system. "Our task now is to build a grassroots movement that puts pressure on every Democrat in Congress to support this legislation because it is the only way to restore balance to the court and protect our democracy."[12]

While Biden and the less radical wing of Congress continued to delay, the pressure from their left flank grew. The "grassroots movement" for court packing was still mostly concentrated in far-left think tanks, newsrooms, and Twitter corners. But these areas drive far too much of the policy conversation among Democrats at our current moment in history, and the idea came to be taken more seriously.

By October, when President Biden's commission turned in its draft findings, the idea had been in the air for months, inching ever closer to the spotlight. Although the results were exactly what he wanted—a group of experts telling the president that this was a very, very bad idea—it didn't matter.

In an article titled "Biden's Supreme Court Commission Successfully Removes Pie from the Sky," Aaron Blake of *The Washington Post* wrote that there was "something to be said for this whole effort potentially moving the Overton Window, a term for the range of politically acceptable ideas. Sometimes pushing extreme measures can be useful politically because it can highlight more-practical ideas that suddenly seem like a valid compromise."[13]

As of this writing, the notion of packing the Court has the support of about half of all Democrats in the United States. When those same voters were asked whether they would support a bill to pack the Court if Joe Biden threw the support of the White House behind it, that number increased to 63 percent. That might not sound like a lot at the moment, but it is much higher than it was when President Roosevelt tried the same thing in the 1930s—and *that* happened before we had massive shadow organizations dumping billions of untraceable dollars into propaganda campaigns to change minds about the issue.

If members of both parties do not step up and vigorously oppose this idea, they might just get away with it this time.

I am not exaggerating when I say that the future of our Constitution is at stake.

CHAPTER EIGHT

Who's Behind This?

O N MARCH 24, 2009, SHORTLY BEFORE I DECIDED TO run for the United States Senate, the Supreme Court convened to hear a case that would come to define American politics for years to come. The plaintiff in the case was a nonprofit organization called *Citizens United*, run at the time by a conservative activist (now a friend of mine) named David Bossie. A few years later, Bossie would become an early political advisor to a brash billionaire from Manhattan named Donald J. Trump. But for the first few decades of his career, he was a congressional investigator, a political activist, and a documentary filmmaker.

In early 2007, when Hillary Clinton was preparing to run for the Democratic presidential nomination against Barack Obama, Bossie and Citizens United made a film titled *Hillary: The Movie*, which painted the candidate in an extremely unflattering light. For the most part, the film was like any other documentary—old footage and ominous music cut with revealing interviews from political commentators and enemies of Hillary Clinton. If you passed it on television, you might not have known whether you were watching a campaign ad or a film.

That, according to the Federal Election Commission, or FEC, was exactly the problem.

At the time, there were specific rules about what kinds of programming you could run on television in the months leading up to a presidential primary. The rules had been put in place to stop the influence of money in politics. The law that enacted these rules was known around Washington as the "McCain-Feingold Act," named after senators John McCain and Russ Feingold. According to these rules, the FEC did allow documentaries and films with a light political spin to run during the primary season; what they did *not* allow was anything that they deemed to be "electioneering," that is, anything that was made for the sole purpose of advocating for or against a particular candidate.

The distinction, as you might imagine, was hazy at best. The Supreme Court had attempted to define it before. In 1976, the Court had ruled in *Buckley* v. *Valeo* that there were "eight magic words" that separated electioneering from mere "issue advocacy." Those words, according to a footnote of the majority opinion in that case, were variations of phrases like "vote for," "cast your ballot for," "defeat," "reject," and things of that nature. As a rule, this didn't give much guidance.

When Bossie and his lawyer had gone to the FEC for an initial ruling, the agency had ruled that *Hillary: The Movie* did qualify as electioneering, and therefore could not lawfully be broadcast during primary season. A federal court in

Washington, DC, had agreed. But the filmmakers obviously did not believe that their film amounted to an "electioneering communication," in the baroque parlance of the federal bureaucracy, a category that typically includes things like short television commercials and flyers taped to telephone poles, and they wanted it to be seen by the largest audience possible.

So they took their case to the Supreme Court, which ultimately agreed to decide the case. Ted Olson, who had been the assistant attorney general under Ronald Reagan and the solicitor general under George W. Bush, represented Citizens United. A veteran Supreme Court practitioner from the solicitor general's office named Malcolm Stewart—who, incidentally, was filling in for Elana Kagan, the future Supreme Court justice who had been Barack Obama's solicitor general for only four days at the time—argued for the executive branch.

What followed was a strange showdown that would affect political campaigns for years.

Standing up at precisely ten o'clock, once the justices had emerged from behind their red velvet curtain, Ted Olson argued first. He argued that in the case before the Court, "freedom [was] being smothered by one of the most complicated, expensive, and incomprehensible regulatory regimes ever invented by the administrative state. In the case that you consider today," he continued, "it is a felony for a small, nonprofit corporation to offer interested viewers a 90-minute political documentary about a candidate for the nation's highest office."[1]

As the argument went on, Olson narrowed his case, claiming that all he had to do to win the case was prove that the FEC's laws did not apply to documentaries such as *Hillary: The Movie*. Like my father and many other solicitors general before him, Olson was above all a lawyer's lawyer, not a politician. He knew how to structure his case so that his client would have the best chance of winning in court. As he took questions from the justices, his years of training became clear. He was setting up the perfect parameters by which his client, Citizens United, could get the victory they were looking for.

When Olson took his seat after making his arguments, Malcolm Stewart, the deputy solicitor general, stepped up to the podium. Although he was not the solicitor general, as an assistant solicitor general, he was still speaking for the government, and thus wore the "morning suit," consisting of a long coat and striped pants that were, and remain, a hallmark tradition of the office. Officially, it was Stewart's job to defend the law and the prior rulings, arguing to the Court that the film was "electioneering" and thus prohibited by the FEC, a federal agency that, in the view of the government, was allowed to police the speech of private American citizens and corporations. It was not an easy case to make, and it was about to get much harder.

During the first few minutes of his oral argument, Stewart

attempted to define the term "express advocacy," which is what *Hillary: The Movie* would have to be defined as if the federal government was going to succeed in banning it. Referring to a previous case, he said that "a court should find that an ad is the functional equivalent of express advocacy only if the ad is susceptible of no reasonable interpretation other than as an appeal to vote for or against a specific candidate."[2]

Almost immediately, Chief Justice John Roberts interrupted him. The two men went back and forth for a few minutes about the proper reading of the relevant precedent. By the second or third question, it was clear that Stewart was unprepared.

This kind of cross-examination, as anyone who has ever argued a case before the Supreme Court can tell you, is the single most daunting thing about presenting a case to the Court. When you argue in a trial court, there is only one judge who can interrupt you to ask questions and challenge you on the integrity of your arguments. In a federal appellate court, you typically argue in front of these judges, although in rare cases it can be more. In the Supreme Court, there are nine, and there is no mechanism for determining when a justice might ask which question, how long you might have to answer them, or in what order the toughest questions might be asked. If you get three minutes into your oral argument and the justices want to spend the remaining twenty-seven talking about a particular word that you used in the second sentence, that is what you're going to do.

To make matters worse, the justices are always prepared. At the level of the Supreme Court, all nine justices will have read the briefs submitted by both parties thoroughly, as well as those submitted by interested parties and other friends of the Court, and they will have gone through potential weaknesses in the cases with their law clerks. When I was a clerk for Justice Alito, the other clerks and I used to spend hours with the briefs, trying to identify holes in arguments and suggest questions that our boss might ask the lawyers arguing before the Court. Some of my fondest memories involve sitting in Justice Alito's office with my co-clerks and parsing the meaning of a particular statute, constitutional provision, or precedent.

After a few questions from Chief Justice Roberts, Justice Alito—who has a unique talent for asking questions during oral arguments that quickly get to the very heart of the case—asked a question. In the opinion of many people who have studied the case in the intervening years, it was this question—the kind of cutting, devastating, seemingly innocent question that forces the person being asked into a tight, inescapable rhetorical corner—that elevated this case from a relatively small statutory dispute into one of the most important cases in the history of electoral politics. It was the kind of question that my fellow law clerks and I came to expect from Justice Alito during oral arguments.

"Do you think," Justice Alito asked, "the Constitution required Congress to draw the line where it did, limiting this to broadcast and cable and so forth? What's your answer to

Mr. Olson's point that there isn't any constitutional difference between the distribution of this movie on video on demand and providing access on the internet, providing DVDs, either through a commercial service or maybe in a public library, proving the same thing in a book? Would the Constitution permit the restriction of all those as well?"

After stammering for a moment, Stewart admitted that this standard "could have been applied to additional media as well."

"You think that if a book was published," Justice Alito said, "a campaign biography that was the functional equivalent of express advocacy, it could be banned?"

From there, it got much worse for the government—much, much worse. Jumping back in, Chief Justice Roberts asked whether, hypothetically, there were "a 500-page book, and at the end it says, 'and so, vote for X,' the government could ban that?"

When Stewart, trying to remain faithful to the government's untenable position, responded in the affirmative, it was clear that this was much more than a simple statutory dispute.

In later years, David Bossie, who ended up prevailing in the case, would cite this line of questioning as the moment he knew the case had enormous implications. In an op-ed in *The Los Angeles Times* from 2016, citing Malcolm Stewart's line about how his standard "could have been applied to other media as well," Bossie asks what, under that "broad interpretation of the law," would have prevented "other forms of speech with corporate ties—books from publishing houses, DVDs from film studios—from being limited during an election cycle if they mentioned or favored a political candidate."[3]

In his book *The Oath*, which includes several chapters on the aftereffects of *Citizens United*, legal analyst Jeffrey Toobin points out the decisive impact of Justice Alito's question on the case.

"Through artful questioning," he writes, "Alito, Kennedy, and Roberts had turned a modestly important case about campaign finance reform into a battle over government censorship."[4]

From there, the case exploded. After the Supreme Court took the extremely rare step of asking both parties to submit new briefs following oral argument, it came to encompass not just the right of a private corporation to broadcast a video, but the question of whether the right of individuals and corporations to donate to political campaigns was protected by the First Amendment. In a 5–4 decision issued on January 21, 2010, the Supreme Court ruled that it was, effectively overturning a great deal of the two thousand or so pages of regulations and analysis that the FEC relied on to make its rulings.

This was a small step in dismantling the administrative state, but it was an important one. It also allowed several candidates who had been having trouble running against the establishment in Washington to get our message out. I was one of them. Marco Rubio, Ron Johnson, Ted Cruz, and Rand Paul were just a few others.

By the time we got to the Senate, however, establishment politicians—especially those on the Left—were furious about the decision. In their minds, *Citizens United* posed an immediate threat to sound government and democracy. There were speeches, op-eds, and long investigative pieces written about the pervasive influence that a sudden influx of cash might have on American politics.

On January 27, 2010, less than a week after the decision was handed down, President Obama addressed these fears in his State of the Union address.

"With all due deference to the separation of powers," he said, "last week the Supreme Court reversed a century of law that I believe will open the floodgates for special interests, including foreign corporations, to spend without limit in our elections. I don't think American elections should be bankrolled by America's most powerful interests, or, worse, by foreign entities. They should be decided by the American people. And I'd urge Democrats and Republicans to pass a bill that helps to correct some of these problems."[5]

Upon hearing those words, Justice Alito shook his head and mouthed the words "not true." This put him on just about every television screen in the nation for a few days. As someone who worked with him for two years, as he served on two different courts, I'm sure this isn't something that he enjoyed. Justice Alito, like many of his predecessors on the Supreme Court, is a lawyer at heart, and in every way, he is exactly the kind of person who should be on the high Court. He considers it his obligation to find the right answer in each case, is willing to do the hard work necessary to find it, and has no desire whatsoever to be in the political spotlight.

He was also absolutely correct. The *Citizens United* decision did not give foreign corporations the right to spend without limit in our elections. Nor did it "open the floodgates" for the rich to buy our elections. It only dismantled a great deal of overly burdensome regulations, allowing the American people to support their chosen candidates without government interference.

In a sense, the fight ended there. President Obama seemed to sense that he had gone too far in attacking the Supreme Court, as I'm sure most of the negative press coverage made clear. It's also worth noting that he did not propose adding justices to the Supreme Court in the hope that he might get *Citizens United* overturned.

That would come later.

Still, for the remainder of his presidency, the Left took this narrative and ran with it. In October of 2010, an advocacy group called the Sunlight Foundation coined the term "dark money," which described funds that had been donated to political campaigns by various nonprofit entities that did not have to disclose the identities of their donors.[6] This, according to critics, would allow corporations to give unlimited money to candidates without having to disclose the source of the funding. In 2016, just a few months after President Trump was elected, a reporter from the *New Yorker* named Jane Mayer published a book about the phenomenon entitled *Dark Money*, which sought to unmask the influence of billionaires such as Charles and David Koch on the rise of what Mayer called "the radical right."[7]

By the time the book was published, the name had become a catch-all term for any donations that supported Republican candidates of any kind. The press spoke in apocalyptic terms about right-wing millionaires and billionaires pulling the strings to get their favored candidates elected. In November of 2018, during the heat of Robert Mueller's investigation into what turned out to be nothing more than a Democratic-run disinformation campaign, Joe Biden wrote an op-ed titled "Foreign Dark Money Is Threatening American Democracy," making explicit parallels between the money that he imagined was being "channeled into U.S. politics."

The evidence for his claim was virtually nonexistent.

"We don't know how much illicit money enters the United States from abroad or how much dark money enters American political campaigns," he wrote. "But in 2015, the Treasury Department estimated that $300 billion is laundered through the U.S. every year. If even a small fraction of that ends up in our political campaigns, it constitutes an unacceptable national security risk."[8]

In court, a judge would be right to reject such evidence as being highly speculative. The justifications that others on the Left were giving for their dire concerns about dark money were similarly unconvincing.

Within two years, however, Biden seemed to have changed his mind about "dark money" in presidential elections. So had most of the liberals who supported him—at least according to the numbers.

In January of 2021, shortly after Biden was inaugurated, *Bloomberg News* conducted a study on the influence that so-called "dark money" groups had had on the 2020 election. What they found was surprising, especially given the rhetoric of Democrats over the previous four years.

"Biden's winning campaign," the report said, "was backed by $145 million in so-called dark money donations, a type of fundraising Democrats have decried for years…The amount of dark money dwarfs the $28.4 million spent on behalf of his rival, former President Donald Trump…Democrats have said they want to ban dark money as uniquely corrupting, since it allows supporters to quietly back a candidate without scrutiny. Yet in their effort to defeat Trump in 2020, they embraced it."[9]

So that means that the Biden campaign took in *four times* more money during the 2020 election than Donald Trump did, all of it coming from innocuously named nonprofit organizations and progressive foundations. For the most part, when you look up these organizations online, you'll see bland, leftist policy proposals. They want to legalize marijuana, protect the climate, and, ironically, get dark money out of politics.

But that's not all.

They want to pack the Supreme Court, too.

———

In many ways, presidential campaigns are like businesses. They consist of different employees that serve different functions; they have office space; they have a definite organizational structure and sources of funding. What's different about them, though, is that after a few months, they go out of business. When the election is over, the winning campaign gets to work moving its employees over to the federal government, effectively staffing another, much bigger business with the employees of their last one.

Losing campaigns, on the other hand, simply cease to exist. They leave thousands of young, politically engaged men and women—some of whom believed, right up until the votes were done being counted on election night, that they might be getting jobs in the White House—out on the street to look for work.

When this happened to the Clinton campaign in 2016, the crash was especially hard. Nearly everyone on that campaign had been dead certain that their candidate was going to win the Oval Office. When she didn't, they scattered. Some of them got jobs covering politics on CNN; others found work on congressional campaigns. Some of them, however, grew energized, channeling their hatred of Donald Trump into a radical fervor for their pet causes.

Among the latter group was Brian Fallon, who had served as Hillary Clinton's national press secretary during the campaign. Before that, he had done the same job for my colleague Chuck Schumer in the Senate. For a while, his reputation around Washington, DC, was stellar. He was, according to a lengthy profile in the *Daily Beast*, "one of the most sought-after operatives in Democratic politics: a brass knuckle brawler with experience at the highest levels of government, a cell-phone filled with the top journalists in town, and a reputation for being preternaturally on message."[10]

But according to the piece, titled "How Hillary Clinton's Press Secretary Self-Radicalized and Became a Resistance Leader," something changed in Fallon after Clinton's loss to Donald Trump. He became less interested in traditional politics, giving up a role as a commentator on CNN, and more interested in ways of putting pressure on Democrats to take radical action. By 2018, two years into President Trump's first term, Fallon and his friends in Democratic politics had seen some of their party's core ideas repudiated time and time again at the ballot box. They had lost the game of electoral politics.

So, they figured, they would change the rules of the game to give themselves a better chance of winning.

In 2018, urged, according to *The New York Times*, by political consultants such as John Podesta, Fallon started Demand Justice, a group whose mission, at least on its face, was to stop President Trump from making more judicial appointments. After two years in the White House, President Trump had already nominated a record number of judges to the federal bench, and he wasn't slowing down anytime soon. But soon, other, more radical ideas began taking over—one in particular.

In October of 2018, following the confirmation of Justice Brett Kavanaugh, academics Mark Tushnet and Laurence Tribe announced their support for the "1.20.21 Project," which aimed to pack four additional justices onto the Supreme Court following their hoped-for inauguration of a Democrat president that year. They made no secret of the partisan nature of the project, claiming they were acting in response to "Republican obstruction, theft and procedural abuse" in the judicial system. The idea still isn't in the mainstream yet. At the time, even the Associated Press described Tribe and Tushnet as "a couple of liberal Harvard law professors."[11] But like a virus infecting a new host, the Court-packing plan became more powerful when it entered the political bloodstream.

As Democrats geared up for their 2020 presidential primary, Demand Justice and other groups like it, such as Take Back the Court and Indivisible, began floating the idea of Court packing as a response to President Trump's judicial nominations. They also began ranking lawmakers on how opposed they were to President Trump's nominees, grading them on a scale of A, meaning they had supported zero of the judges that President Trump had nominated, to F, which meant that they had supported some.

By 2019, *The Washington Post* observed: "The once-remote idea of adding more justices to the Supreme Court to change its ideological bent is prompting growing discussion within the Democratic Party, creating a new frontier for presidential candidates looking to display their liberal credentials." That March, former Attorney General Eric Holder threw his weight behind the idea: "We should be talking even about expanding the number of people who serve on the Supreme Court," he said, "if there is a Democratic president and a Congress that would do that."[12] At least he was being honest in describing the plan as nothing more than a partisan power grab.

In this new radicalized landscape, old loyalties didn't matter. Shortly after setting up shop, Demand Justice gave Chuck Schumer, Brian Fallon's old boss, a "C" grade for having the nerve to do his duty according to the Constitution and confirm a few of President Trump's judicial nominees. Shortly afterward, according to the *Daily Beast*, the two stopped speaking.

The group also posted messages and sent out email blasts that accused President Trump of "packing the Court" with Republican nominees, making the case that the only way to stop it was to add justices to the Supreme Court. In March 2019, Brian Fallon declared: "We don't consider those two seats that Trump has filled"—Gorsuch and Kavanaugh—"to be legitimate."[13] In order to get the message out, Demand Justice hired some of the most sought-after Democrats in Washington. For a time, Jen Psaki, who would go on to become Joe Biden's press secretary, was an outside advisor to Demand Justice. They also hired Paige Herwig, who is now, according to Fox News, "Biden's point person on judicial nominations."[14] To clarify: a liberal activist whose most recent job was advising a group that sought to dismantle the Supreme Court by filling it with radical liberal justices is now in charge of helping the president of the United States select judicial nominees. In other words, this strange fantasy of the Left is back with a vengeance, and we are closer than we've ever been to seeing it become a reality.

In principle, the situation was no different than it had been for President Franklin Delano Roosevelt in the 1930s. In the aftermath of a crisis, a liberal president was trying to take unprecedented control of the federal government. He also feared that some of his party's most treasured legislative objectives might be in danger of being declared unconstitutional by the Supreme Court. He knew that with the Court as it was currently configured, with a majority of justices who would adhere to the words of the Constitution as written, he wasn't likely to get the rulings that he wanted. Such a Supreme Court was not likely, for example, to uphold a law mandating vaccines for all federal employees—or for all American citizens, for that matter—because that would be a gross violation of the Constitution.

So that president listened to the most radical voices around him and made plans to add enough justices to the Court so that he could get the rulings he was looking for.

But this time, it was much different. First of all, the voices in the president's ear were backed by billions of dollars, most of it given to shady groups in a panic during the presidency of Donald Trump. There is no way to trace who's giving it, and there is no sign that it's going to stop coming anytime soon. Demand Justice, for instance, is linked to the Sixteen Thirty Fund, which, according to Fox News, is "a nonprofit incubator that provides its tax and legal status to nonprofits, which allows them to avoid filing publicly available tax forms. The Sixteen Thirty Fund is managed by the Washington,

D.C.-based consulting firm Arabella Advisors, which oversees a large network that pulled in $715 million in secretive donations for left-wing groups and causes it houses in 2019 alone."[15]

Second, it was more blatant than ever. When President Roosevelt first floated the idea of Court packing, he knew that the idea of a political Supreme Court would be politically toxic. Even the least engaged citizens would be able to tell that something was off about it. So FDR and his associates lied. They said that the reason they were packing the Court had nothing to do with politics; it was, they said, all about the "Nine Old Men" of the Court. They were simply too old to keep up with their work, and they needed to be replaced by newer, more agile, young justices. In large part, it was the public's ability to sniff out this blatant lie from the beginning that stopped the Court-packing bill from getting out of the Senate—but, as we've seen, it was also a series of accidents that could not possibly be repeated.

This time, the liberal interest groups were not pretending. They were coming out and saying that the Supreme Court was too "conservative" for them, and that they needed to tip things in a more liberal direction. During the Democratic primary debates, which occurred about a year before Joe Biden realized that he was going to need money from these groups if he stood any chance of winning, this had been a common refrain. At some point during the four years that Donald Trump was in office, it had become perfectly fine not only to say that the

Supreme Court was a political body, but also to insist that we as a country needed to do something about it.

"With a 6-3 Republican supermajority," reads a current page on the website of Demand Justice that asks for donations, "the Supreme Court is too biased in favor of special interests and Republican politicians. Our democracy is at risk from decisions that suppress the right to vote. Adding four seats is the solution—and we need your help to get it done. Congress can change the number of justices on the Court at any time with a simple piece of legislation, and it has done so many times throughout American history."[16]

There it is, out in the open.

They are not waiting around, either. In an article in *The New York Times* about the potential that Democrats in the Senate, with an average age of sixty-four, might get sick or die and thus be unable to vote, Brian Fallon noted that the Democratic majority hangs in a very delicate balance. The loss of one vote might sink their whole plot before it even gets off the ground.

"Our ability to make good on Biden's agenda," he said, "is pretty much dangling by a thread. I don't think it's uncouth to talk about it. I think it's a reality that has to inform the urgency with which we approach those issues."[17]

By this point, of course, "Biden's agenda" has very little to do with the president himself. It's not even *his* agenda, technically speaking. It includes policies that he has repudiated for decades, even as recently as the Democratic primary debates.

Rather, it is the agenda of the radical Left, which now has full control of the federal government. Through a concentrated publicity campaign funded largely by shadowy billionaire donors, these activists have worked behind the scenes throughout the entire Trump presidency to sow discord and paint the Supreme Court as an overwhelmingly partisan, bitter place, one that is in need of emergency packing in order to save democracy.

Sadly, it is working. A few months after Biden's Supreme Court commission had released its draft findings, it would become clear that the "Overton Window," to use the phrase referenced by Aaron Blake in *The Washington Post*, had moved several miles to the left. Almost as soon as the commission's official report was released, many of the people who'd been involved in writing it went rogue, coming out with op-eds and public statements of their own that seemed to contradict the commission's official findings. Perhaps they felt emboldened by how mainstream the idea had become thanks to the sudden proliferation of dark money.

In early December 2021, Americans were treated to a one-two punch of op-eds by prominent commissioners arguing for a bigger Court. On December 9, *The Washington Post* published one jointly authored by longtime Court-packing advocate Laurence Tribe and retired federal judge Nancy Gertner. Back in 2018, Tribe had argued that modern attempts to pack the Court were distinct from Roosevelt's because today's push "stems from Republican actions, not the court's decisions"—as if the blatant partisanship somehow made it more legitimate.[18]

Tribe became something of a leftist gadfly during the Trump years, known for posting outrageous, histrionic claims about the Trump administration on Twitter. BuzzFeed News— hardly a right-wing outlet—ran a story about "prominent liberals…sharing unconfirmed, speculative, and sometimes wild information" as part of an "information echo chamber…in which anti-Trump public figures share unreliable information, the very act of which the sources of these reports use to bolster their own legitimacy." BuzzFeed noted: "Perhaps no one embodies this trend so well as Laurence Tribe," who had breathlessly shared a baseless allegation that Trump paid $10 million to a member of Congress to leak a letter from FBI Director James Comey.[19] The article criticized the wisdom of Tribe using his position as a prominent intellectual to spread misinformation.

Apparently, Tribe learned nothing. His op-ed with Judge Gertner is full of misinformation and attacks not just on the Court but on our constitutional system itself. "In voting to submit the report [of their commission] to the president," the authors declare, "neither of us cast a vote of confidence in the Supreme Court itself." It is unconscionable for a lawyer who has argued before the Supreme Court and a onetime judge in the federal system to say they have no confidence in the nation's highest court. I've disagreed with plenty of Supreme Court decisions, but I've never questioned the legitimacy of the institution. Not once. It shows how far this movement is willing to go.

Tribe and Gertner say the Court has lost their confidence for three reasons: "First, the dubious legitimacy of the way some justices were appointed; second, what Justice Sonia Sotomayor rightly called the "stench" of politics hovering over this court's deliberations about the most contentious issues; and third, the anti-democratic, anti-egalitarian direction of this court's decisions about matters such as voting rights, gerrymandering and the corrupting effects of dark money."

They don't provide any evidence to back up their claims of justices being appointed with "dubious legitimacy." But we can assume they are referring to the appointments of Justices Gorsuch, Kavanaugh, and Barrett during the Trump administration. They're parroting the Demand Justice view, whose leader said they didn't consider Trump's appointments legitimate. Tribe and Gertner don't attempt to explain exactly *how* they're illegitimate. That's because the Left's logic behind this claim is, shall we say, confused. They may still believe that President Trump was not legitimately elected (Tribe has been known to push conspiracy theories about this) and therefore no appointments made by his administration should count. Or, they may be upset about the Senate declining to confirm President Obama's nominee, Merrick Garland, in 2016. This was a Senate procedural issue—simply put, the Senate does not have to confirm every nominee the President nominates.

For Tribe and Gertner to cite Justice Sotomayor's concern

about the "stench" of politics over Court decisions as they argue for a more partisan Court is so ironic, so lacking in self-awareness, that it's hardly worth considering. The Left, of course, believes their use of political power to be righteous and good, while the Right doing so is evil.

Finally, they accuse the Court of being "anti-democratic" and "anti-egalitarian." What they, and so many on the Left don't understand, is that we don't live in a pure democracy. The founders didn't set things up that way. Our Constitution gives our democracy some checks, and one of these is our judicial system, the highest point of which is the Supreme Court. The Court's job is to interpret our laws and thereby set limits on what government can or can't do, according to the Constitution. Rulings that go against certain Democratic priorities like lessening election protections and limiting political speech is not, itself, "anti-democratic" action. Sometimes that means serving as a buffer against majoritarian impulses, against rank democracy and the passions of the day, to maintain faithfulness to the Constitution. As an institution, the Court is only as "democratic" or "anti-democratic," as "egalitarian" or "anti-egalitarian," as the parameters of the Constitution allow it to be. Liberals have a hard time accepting this perhaps because, like Woodrow Wilson, they think they know better than the Constitution.

Tribe and Gertner's solution is "offsetting the way the Court has been 'packed' in an anti-democratic direction with added appointments leaning the other way." The concerns about the "stench of politics" seem to have evaporated. They try to argue that the Court was "packed" with conservatives by Trump, but that is ultimately a failed attempt to "own" the term. All of Trump's nominees were—whether Democrats like it or not—nominated and confirmed according to the process set down by the Constitution and the rules of the Senate. Even in Merrick Garland's case, the process was carried out according to Senate procedure. To add additional justices to the Supreme Court is not the same thing as working within the bounds of present procedure, and it is disingenuous to pretend otherwise.

The day after Tribe and Gertner's piece appeared saw a dramatic twist that might seem fabricated if it weren't completely verifiable. Another commissioner published an op-ed in *Time* magazine on December 10: Kermit Roosevelt III, a lawyer, law professor, and distant cousin of the original would-be Court-packer President Franklin Delano Roosevelt.

The younger Roosevelt claimed that, contrary to what his report had said, packing the Court was essential. "I spent the last seven months on President Biden's Supreme Court commission, talking, listening, and sometimes arguing with experts from a variety of legal backgrounds...I went into the process thinking that the system was working but that improvements were possible. I came out scared."[20]

Roosevelt outlines some usual talking points that had been handed out by groups like Demand Justice. His main criticism is that the Court has become too political, and only packing can fix this. But his argument is severely flawed. "The Framers intended that the American people, through the elections of presidents and senators, would have ultimate, though indirect, control of the composition of the Supreme Court," he points out. So far, so good. "But the Framers did not anticipate the party system, and that throws a wrench in the works." This is simply not correct. Perhaps Professor Roosevelt should audit an undergraduate American history class at the University of Pennsylvania, where he teaches.

Factions and parties were absolutely known to the Framers. Members of the British Parliament, which controlled the American Colonies before independence, were grouped into parties. For instance, Lord North, the Prime Minister who presided over the War of Independence was a Tory. Edmund Burke, who was more sympathetic to the American cause, was a Whig. At the Constitutional Convention the founders were divided into the Federalist and Anti-Federalist factions. George Washington would not have warned against factionalism in his farewell address if he didn't think it existed. But despite Washington's warnings, political parties are a common feature in free societies and America was no exception. Every president from Jefferson onward has essentially been a member of a party.

To claim the political parties weren't a consideration of the founders is naïve at best and disingenuous at worst. But Professor Roosevelt uses this argument to attack the Electoral College and equal representation in the Senate—two favorite targets of the modern Left, who would like to get rid of the Electoral College and turn the Senate into another version of the House. He reasons: "A president elected by a minority of the people can nominate judges who are then confirmed by Senators representing a minority of the people." In 1992, Bill Clinton won 43 percent of the popular vote (less than President Trump's 46 percent in 2016). The following year, he nominated Ruth Bader Ginsburg to the Supreme Court, and she was confirmed by a Senate with equal representation from each state. I wonder if Professor Roosevelt considers her appointment legitimate.

The example he gives as a major political problem facing the Court is abortion. At least he's honest about that. But while he, like Tribe and Gertner, claims the Court has labeled "anti-democratic," he fails to consider that the decision in *Roe* v. *Wade* was itself an anti-democratic action. It contravened laws passed by democratically elected state governments that restricted abortion. Note that since that decision in 1973, while conservatives have fought courageously to get it overturned, it was never seriously suggested that any Republican president add Supreme Court justices during his term to accomplish that goal.

Professor Roosevelt suggested term limits for justices as a possible solution, but I think he knows that isn't workable. He goes all-in on Court packing, because, as he sees it: "the Republican Party [is] attacking democracy, and the Supreme Court is helping it. Because it is [a] partisan phenomenon, there is no nonpartisan good-government fix for it." Actually, the good-government fix is, as always, to follow the Constitution, but he has confused "good government" with "Democrats getting what they want." What he decries as a "minoritarian takeover" is, in fact, protection from a "majoritarian takeover." The tension between the minority and the majority is a feature in the government the founders designed, not a bug to be squashed—in true Roosevelt fashion—with the exercise of raw political power.

Shortly afterward, Senator Elizabeth Warren wrote her own op-ed on the subject, effectively declaring that no matter what the Supreme Court commission decided, she was going to push for the idea.

"With each move," Senator Warren wrote in the *Boston Globe*, "the court shows why it's important to restore America's faith in an independent judiciary committed to the rule of law. To do that, I believe it's time for Congress to yet again use its constitutional authority to expand the number of justices on the Supreme Court. I don't come to this conclusion lightly or because I disagree with a particular decision; I come to this conclusion because I believe the current court threatens the democratic foundations of our nation."[21]

Coming from a disgruntled professor or an activist, this might not have meant much. But from a United States senator who mounted a serious campaign for the presidency and retains an enormous amount of influence in the Democratic Party, it means a whole lot. If nothing else, the endorsement from Senator Warren shows that the efforts of these dark money groups have paid off in spades, convincing the mainstream members of the Democratic Party that the Overton Window on Court packing is moving, and that they need to run with it if they have any hope of being reelected.

As of right now, the number of Democrats in Congress willing to support Court packing is relatively small, but it's growing every day. It may take just a few more decisions that don't go their way to turn the rest of them.

CHAPTER NINE

What's at Stake?

O N December 1, 2021, crowds came from all over the country to protest in front of the Supreme Court. In what has become an all too common sight over the past few years, they arranged themselves into two separate camps. On one side, there were people who wanted the Court to overturn *Roe* v. *Wade*, the decision that effectively created a constitutional right to on-demand abortion. This group included pro-life activists, religious leaders, and even a few government officials who had come to show their support.

On the other side, there were pro-abortion activists. They were as diverse as the first group, and equally as passionate. They held signs with slogans such as "Abortion Is Essential" and "Bans off Our Bodies." Loud music blared from speakers, and several people at once attempted to give speeches via megaphones. In the front of the crowd, likenesses of the heads of all nine Supreme Court justices floated on wooden sticks, held aloft by women who'd covered themselves in black for the occasion. Photojournalists and camera crews made their way through the crowd, crouching to get the best footage for that evening's broadcasts and pictures for the next morning's newspapers.

They weren't disappointed.

At 7:45 a.m., according to *The Washington Post*, four abortion-rights activists stood as close to the Supreme Court as they were allowed and swallowed pills, making a show of it for the gathering news crews. The pill was a drug called mifepristone, often taken to end pregnancy without an abortion procedure. None of these women was pregnant, according to a spokesperson for the group *Shout Your Abortion*, which helped organize the protests. In an interview with *The Washington Post*, she said that the whole exercise had been staged to "[usher] in a new paradigm" that would allow women to have such "abortion pills" delivered directly to their mailboxes, effectively bypassing any state laws that might outlaw the practice in the future.[1]

Over the next few hours, the demonstrations only grew more extreme. The protestors inched closer to one another and screamed their prewritten slogans in each other's faces; several smaller groups broke off and tried to form tight circles around people, attempting to intimidate them into silence. By the end of the morning, the United States Capitol Police would arrest 33 people for blocking First Street, which was busy, given that it was a Wednesday morning.

Inside the Supreme Court, the case on the docket was *Dobbs v. Jackson Women's Health Organization*, which involved the validity of a Mississippi law that would ban all abortions after fifteen weeks of pregnancy. For months, there had been newspaper editorials and talking heads on television warning that the case would place the right to an abortion in the United States in jeopardy.

Again, these pieces spoke of [and to] the Supreme Court as if it were a political body, where public opinion plays a legitimate role, and the loudest voices often prevail. The coverage suggested a world in which the protestors who'd gathered outside would have some effect on what was going on inside the courtroom.

But they would not.

That day, all they could do was listen.

At precisely ten o'clock, much of the noise stopped. After a few seconds of crackling from the speakers, the voice of the Supreme Court marshal began filling the air, introducing the justices and signaling that oral arguments were about to begin. This was a big change. For most of its history, the Supreme Court heard oral arguments in front of a relatively small audience. Only the people in the courtroom, meaning a maximum of a few hundred people at a time since 1935, and a tiny fraction of that before then, could perceive in real time what the lawyers were saying, what questions were being asked of them, and how the justices seemed to be reacting to each assertion. Written transcripts have been made available to the public without change on the day of argument since the Court's 2006 term, but transcripts, while useful in their own right, have no way of communicating volume, intensity, intonation, and other, more subtle signals. And although the Court began making audio recordings of oral arguments in 1955, prior to 2010 they were not made available until the beginning of the Court's next term (each term begins on the first Monday in October), and the process of obtaining them was typically expensive and time consuming. From 2010 until 2020, the audio recordings of these proceedings were posted on the Courts website every Friday, which was fantastic. But even then there was a delay of a few days between each argument and the release of the recording.

Then, when the COVID-19 pandemic began, the justices were forced to work from home like the rest of us. In a sense, this was a return to the very early years of the Supreme Court, when the justices *had* no building in which to gather, and thus conducted most of their business from home. But by the time the pandemic arrived in 2020, we had the internet and Zoom meetings, allowing the justices—and, for the first time ever, anyone in the world with an internet connection—to attend the oral arguments virtually. So, for the first time ever, the door of the Supreme Court was thrown wide open to anyone who wanted to listen, allowing them to give their reactions and opinions on what was happening in real time.

For the most part, this was an interesting experiment. It also allowed the world to get a glimpse into just how arguments before the Court work, albeit in slightly different form. During the pandemic, due to the restrictive nature of Zoom meetings, the justices could no longer interrupt lawyers at will; they had to wait to be called on by the chief justice before they could speak. But by and large, the public liked the access. Studies show that during the pandemic, as many as 500,000 people around the country tuned into the Court's proceedings, and close to 1.9 million listened to at least one oral argument session.

So, when the Supreme Court resumed its in-person work

in Cass Gilbert's massive temple of the law, they kept that metaphorical door open, broadcasting their arguments in real time over phones and the internet. But this was the only one of the COVID protocols that remained. Everything else went back to normal after COVID. Justices were back in their high-backed leather seats, the lawyers were back at their podiums, and the justices were once again able to interrupt, examine, and interrogate the lawyers as they pleased. Only now they were doing it with an audience of hundreds of thousands.

On December 1, 2021, several of the justices seemed well aware of this—perhaps almost *too* aware.

For a while, things proceeded as usual. Scott Stewart, the solicitor general of Mississippi, stepped up to the podium and began articulating arguments on behalf of his state. The first lines of his argument were among the most forceful that have ever been uttered in defense of the right to life—at least, they're the most forceful words on the subject that have been uttered in the chamber of the Supreme Court for a very long time.

"*Roe versus Wade* and *Planned Parenthood versus Casey* haunt our country," he said. At these first few words alone, the pro-life crowds outside erupted into applause. There was a similar reaction from the pro-abortion crowd, which contained a fair amount of obscenity and went on for longer. But Stewart, safe from the weight of public opinion in the grand chamber of the Court, continued.

"They have no basis in the Constitution. They have no home in our history or traditions. They've damaged the democratic process. They've poisoned the law. They've choked off compromise. For fifty years, they've kept this court at the center of a political battle that it can never resolve. And fifty years on, they stand alone. Nowhere else does this court recognize a right to end human life."[2]

For a few seconds, he outlined the law, explicitly asking that the Supreme Court take the rare step of overturning two of its most public and contentious decisions. This was a pivotal moment for the Supreme Court, and one that many pro-life advocates have been waiting to experience for a long time.

Roe v. *Wade* was decided when I was only seventeen months old. I've known what it meant for most of my life. When I was about ten, my dad sat me down and explained the decision to me. I reacted by telling him that it seemed doubly problematic, because abortion policy should be a matter of state law rather than federal, to be decided by legislatures rather than judges. My dad was a genuinely happy person—one with a wide range of interests and boundless intellectual curiosity—but he seemed especially delighted by that answer. But not too long after that conversation, I got a firsthand look at how personal the Left intended to make their fight.

One Saturday morning when I was eleven, an entire busload of abortion-rights protestors showed up in front of our house and, without warning or explanation, began picketing on the sidewalk, chanting "keep your laws off our bodies" over and over again. This seemed strange development in our quiet neighborhood, and it truly was. It was made even more strange by the fact that I was witnessing this unexpected performance alone (the only other person home at that moment was my sister Wendy, then a teenager, who somehow managed to sleep until almost noon that day). I was fascinated by the commotion, and—after a brief moment imagining what might happen if I decided to turn the hose on them or deploy my secret stash of fireworks to disperse the crowd (I quickly decided that would be a big mistake)—I went outside to talk to the protesters. The moment I matter-of-factly introduced myself to the woman who appeared to be in charge—let's call her Karen—she addressed me, in the most demeaning tone imaginable, saying: "Hello, little boy. We're not here to hurt you, we just disagree with some of the things your daddy has been doing at the Supreme Court." The "we're not here to hurt you" stuck with me. And yet, here they were at the residence of a public official, making sure he knew that they knew where he, his wife, and his children lived, ate, played, and slept every night. Eventually, Karen and her friends got bored, retreated to their bus, and then abruptly left. My parents pulled up no more than thirty seconds after the bus drove away and asked if I knew anything about the big bus they'd just seen pulling out of our neighborhood. I had quite a story for them.

Living with bad precedent like *Roe* and *Planned Parenthood v. Casey*—which essentially upheld *Roe*'s central holding—for so long has been discouraging, and at times the idea of it ever being overturned has seemed quite distant. It's especially frustrating because if ten-year-old me could see that the *Roe* decision had shaky legal grounding, surely lots of other people could too. And many did. In fact, many of the people who liked the outcome of that case have admitted that it was, in the immortal and always colloquial words of Justice Antonin Scalia, "a lousy opinion." Do you suppose that thought ever occurred to Karen?

Even Ruth Bader Ginsburg, one of the most "liberal" justices in the history of the Supreme Court, had admitted repeatedly that *Roe* v. *Wade* rested on shaky legal reasoning. In March of 1993, speaking shortly after the Supreme Court's ruling in *Planned Parenthood* v. *Casey*, she devoted an entire lecture at New York University to the subject, enumerating various ways in which basing a right to abortion on some imagined, constitutional right to "privacy" (entirely distinct from the privacy interests protected by the Fourth Amendment, and yet articulated nowhere in that or any other provision of the constitution) was not only incorrect, but dangerous. In later years, Justice Ginsburg would confront the ugly—and, in the estimation of several historians, racist—roots of the abortion-rights movement itself, admitting that at the time *Roe* v. *Wade* was decided, "there was a concern about population growth and particularly growth in populations that we didn't want to have too many of."[3]

But for the most part, her concern with the Supreme Court's stance on abortion wasn't moral. Indeed, she continued to be a supporter of a woman's right to have an abortion until the day she died. Her concern, rather, was about the way that in one single "breathtaking" opinion, decided by a very small group of people, the Supreme Court had "fashioned a set of rules that displaced virtually every state law then in force."[4] She, like all good justices on the Supreme Court, knew that "doctrinal limbs too swiftly constructed," to adapt the words of her 1992 lecture, "may prove unstable."[5]

In a sense, all that Scott Stewart and the state of Mississippi were doing on December 1 was agreeing with her. They were not attempting to make abortion illegal throughout the entire United States, as some news sources might have had you believe. They were not even attempting to make all abortion illegal in the state of Mississippi—*could* not, in fact, have done so even if they wanted to. They were only attempting to return the Supreme Court to its previously held belief that the Constitution does not say anything on the subject of abortion, and that abortion is therefore an issue that should be left to the states to decide through the mechanism of democratic choice, the same way the states decide thousands of other pressing issues every day.

Midway through the argument, Justice Sonia Sotomayor, seeming to speak more to the audience of activists outside than to the quiet, interested parties inside, launched into a speech about how a reversal of *Roe* v. *Wade* would make the Supreme Court seem "political," wondering aloud whether the Court would ever "survive the stench" of hearing the current case. She also dedicated a few minutes to a comparison between living fetuses and dead bodies, pointing out that there are about "forty percent of dead people who, if you touch their feet, the foot will recoil."[6]

But all that was a distraction from the main issue, which was whether or not the Supreme Court—which, for the first time in many years, contained a majority committed to interpreting the Constitution according to the original meaning of the words therein—would overrule one of the worst decisions in the history of the institution. Despite the protests raging outside, this was not a political decision, and it had very little to do with the content of the state law itself.

During the oral arguments of Solicitor General Elizabeth Prelogar (representing the Biden administration), Justice Alito asked the question that had been lingering around the *Roe* v. *Wade* decision for years. The exchange is telling, and it goes to the very heart of the case.

JUSTICE ALITO: Is it your argument that a case can never be overruled simply because it was egregiously wrong?

GENERAL PRELOGAR: I think that at the very least, the state would have to come forward with some kind of materially changed circumstance or some kind of materially new argument, and Mississippi hasn't done so in this case...

JUSTICE ALITO: Really? So suppose *Plessy versus Ferguson* was re-argued in 1897, so nothing had changed. Would it not be sufficient to say that was an egregiously wrong decision on the day it was handed down, and now it should be overruled?

GENERAL PRELOGAR: It certainly was egregiously wrong on the day that it was handed down, *Plessy*, but what the

Court said in analyzing *Plessy* to *Brown* and *Casey* was that what had become clear is that the factual premise that underlay the decision, this idea that segregation didn't create a badge of inferiority, had been entirely mistaken...

JUSTICE ALITO: Is it your answer that we needed all the experience from 1896 to 1954 to realize that *Plessy* was—was wrongly decided? Would you answer my question? Had it come before the Court in 1897, should it have been overruled or not?

GENERAL PRELOGAR: I think it should have been overruled, but I think that the factual premise was wrong in the moment it was decided, and the Court realized that and clarified that when it overruled in *Brown*.

JUSTICE ALITO: So there are...circumstances in which a decision may be overruled, properly overruled, when it must be overruled simply because it was egregiously wrong at the moment it was decided?

The solicitor general did not respond to the final question—which is itself stunning—but the answer was clear to everyone listening. The legal reasoning in *Roe* v. *Wade* was bad from the beginning, and it remained bad every time it was upheld. The only problem was that in the years between then and now, the Supreme Court has been filled with justices who see it as their duty not to read and interpret the Constitution, but to twist it and read between its lines in order to create the rights they would like to be in it.

There is nothing wrong with overturning a bad decision. The Supreme Court has done it many times during its history, most notably in *Brown* v. *Board of Education*, which held that the Court had been dead wrong when it ruled in *Plessy* v. *Ferguson* that "separate but equal" was perfectly fine as long as the facilities for Black people and white people were comparable. Under the very same objections that the Biden administration was raising in this case, however, the Warren Court would have been stuck with *Plessy* on the grounds that it had been settled law for far too long.

As of this writing, a decision in *Dobbs* v. *Jackson Women's Health Organization* has not yet been rendered. We do not know whether the Supreme Court will rule to overturn *Roe* v. *Wade* or not. But we know a few things from the oral arguments. The first is that despite enormous political pressure from the outside—and some unusual signals of defensiveness from some of the more liberal justices on the Court—the argument went exactly as it should have. Both sides presented arguments, and they were questioned by the justices about the validity of those arguments. The Biden administration argued that *Roe* v. *Wade* should stand because it has been the law for decades, just as a lawyer in the early twentieth century might have argued that *Plessy* v. *Ferguson* was settled law.

Only time will tell whether the Supreme Court will deem this argument sufficient to strike down the Mississippi law. I know my opinion on the subject, of course, and that is that *Roe* v. *Wade* was incorrectly decided and that it should be overturned at the earliest opportunity. I know exactly how *I* would rule if I were a member of the Court.

But I am not. Right now, the American judicial system is working imperfectly at times, but on the whole, it's functioning exceptionally well. There are nine justices working on this case, who are oath-bound to decide the case correctly. The Court's ruling—whenever it may emerge, whatever it may be, and whether I like it or not—will stand. If pro-life Americans like me don't like the ruling, I'm sure we will be disappointed, but then go back to strategizing as we have for years to find ways to protect the unborn without undermining our judicial system as a whole. But if the pro-abortion Left doesn't like the decision, we might soon find ourselves in the midst of a constitutional crisis.

As we have already seen, the stage has been set for an invasion of the Supreme Court. There is money pouring in from progressive organizations all over the place. Those organizations are pressuring Democratic lawmakers to attack the judiciary. Their stated goal is to increase the size of the Supreme Court from nine justices to thirteen or more. As of this moment, public opinion is against them. But they are well aware that if they can convince enough Americans that the Supreme Court has acquired, in the words of Justice Sonia Sotomayor, the "stench" of politics, then they might be able to convince enough of them that this insane idea is a good one.

At the moment, the Biden administration is using the threat of Court packing in much the same way that President Franklin Roosevelt did in 1937. He knows that it probably won't work, and that the American people would almost certainly oppose any legislation he or members of his party might propose to pack the Court. But he also knows that the justices themselves do not want it to get that far. Several of them, including the liberal Justice Stephen Breyer (on his way out the door), have warned against it.

"What goes around comes around," he said during an interview with NPR. "And if Democrats can do it, the Republicans can do it."[7] What he neglects to mention is that Republicans don't *want* to do it. They never have. During the Obama years, we saw several Supreme Court decisions that did not go our way. I was so incensed by the ruling in *National Federation of Independent Business* v. *Sebelius* that I wrote a book about it. But my colleagues and I did not call for expanding the Supreme Court—because what we care most about is the Constitution, the people it protects, and the continuity of the restrained and balanced government it establishes.

Most of the American public still understands that Court-packing is wrong. But as long as that particular sword is held over the Supreme Court by prominent liberals in and out of government, justices like Sonia Sotomayor will be especially concerned about ruling the way that the radical Left wants them to. If they don't, they know that there might soon be several more chairs behind the bench.

Additionally, given all the protests and media attention that have surrounded the Courts most recent decisions on abortion, a ruling that goes against the wishes of the Left might just move the Overton Window on the Court-packing issue to a place where it is, finally, a viable option.

Speaking outside the Supreme Court on December 1, Brian Fallon of Demand Justice—which is still pumping money into making sure that the effort to pack the Court continues—said, "This push will go into hyperdrive if the court upholds Mississippi's ban, let alone overturns Roe outright."[8]

Of course, if it's not this decision, it could be another one. Unless Americans unite quickly and decisively in opposition to this tragic idea, neither the protests nor the pressure will cease until the damage is finally done. The protests will not stop. The pressure will not stop.

———————

So what is at stake?

To begin, throughout our history there have been dozens of hot-button issues that have come to the public's attention in the context of close Supreme Court decisions—including many important questions regarding religious freedom, gun ownership, and the proper role of the federal government. There will be more in the future.

But those are minor compared to the deeper issue at stake with Court packing.

I'm sure you won't believe me if I tell you that when it comes to Court packing, *everything* is at stake. You've probably heard multiple politicians this week alone tell you that some issue or another is the one that will "define the United States for decades to come," or that the next election is "the most important election of the century," or of your life, or of all time.

In part, that's just how we speak about politics. To a degree, it always has been. But the hyperbole increased during the presidency of Donald Trump, and it has only gotten worse since.

In the case of packing the Supreme Court, however, everything really *is* at stake.

Let me explain. I've already said that President Biden and congressional Democrats have no shortage of bad ideas for this country. In just one year, they have introduced draconian measures that would drastically expand the control that the federal government has over the lives of American citizens.

But when it comes to their outrageous attempts to pack the Supreme Court, they are attacking more than just our individual liberties. They are attacking more than the institution of the Supreme Court. What they are really attacking is the structure of the Constitution itself, which sets up an enormously complex and balanced system of government. The judicial branch in particular has carved out a niche for itself over the years, building centuries of precedent to arrive at a perfectly balanced system for resolving disputes regarding what is and is not constitutional. It is a structure that has never been thoroughly replicated anywhere else in the world, and perhaps never will be. And when it comes to the American system of government, as Justice Antonin Scalia once put it, "structure is everything."[9]

We can talk about rights all day long. We can complain about how different administrations of both major political parties violate them, and we can work together to make sure that those violations cease, with Congress, the presidency, and the courts playing a vital role, and the ultimate backstop residing with voters. But in truth, the protections enumerated in the Bill of Rights we all enjoy as Americans were something of an afterthought. They weren't tacked on to the Constitution until two years after the original document (without amendments) had been written and ratified. What mattered to our founders was setting up a system of government that would last for centuries—one with parts that worked together in an endless sequence of checks and balances, ensuring that power could never become centralized in one person, party, or body.

For centuries, that system has unleashed the greatest wave of human flourishing ever recorded by historians.

If President Biden and the Democrats manage to expand the size of the Supreme Court—that is, if they succeed in increasing the number of seats on the Court—they will effectively be robbing that branch of its power and grabbing it for themselves. It would mean that the United States government would lose its structure—and, as Justice Scalia has reminded us, without that structure, we are nothing.

If any president were to pack the Supreme Court for partisan purposes, that president would delegitimize the Court in the eyes of the American citizenry and of the world. You can't delegitimize the Court without fundamentally threatening and eroding some of our most valued liberties. You can't do that without threatening things like religious freedom, free speech, federalism, and separation of powers—things that are themselves often unpopular but are protected by the Constitution precisely *because* they are unpopular.

And yes, in that respect, the Constitution is sometimes counterdemocratic. It can in some ways even be described as *fundamentally* undemocratic. In fact, that is the whole reason to have one at all—to protect us from the impulse of the majority to harm a few in the name of the many.

Conclusion

Dᴜʀɪɴɢ ᴛʜᴇ Tʀᴜᴍᴘ ᴘʀᴇsɪᴅᴇɴᴄʏ ᴀɴᴅ ɪᴛs ᴀғᴛᴇʀᴍᴀᴛʜ, we were lectured incessantly about Donald Trump's constant "norm busting." We expected that from politicians on the Left, but it was the unceasing media drumbeat that tried to hammer the message home into our brains again and again and again. *The New York Times* decried "Trump's Tradition of Broken Traditions." ABC News told us "How Trump Obliterated Norms and Changed the Presidency." And *The Washington Post* gave us "The Definitive List of the 20 Presidential Norms Trump Broke."

If Democrats—fueled by a media cheering section—decide to expand the Supreme Court, they will lose all credibility in any future discussions about the preservation of norms. If they pack the Court, they will have committed one of the most drastic acts of norm busting in American history, with far greater consequences than anything Trump was accused of doing. Democrats were willing to impeach President Trump over a phone call to Ukraine, but does anyone really think that changing the nature of the highest tribunal in the most powerful nation in the world would not be a much more earth-shattering event?

The norms that would be shattered and otherwise weakened are not just social ones, not just things that have a subtle impact. This particular norm-shattering exercise would essentially change the constitutional structure of our government, even if Democrats purport to leave it intact. The whole point of having a constitution is to limit government power. One of the limits on that power in the Constitution is that the process of changing that document through amendments takes time, and requires building enough political consensus to achieve a supermajority two different ways. Either two-thirds of both houses of Congress can propose an amendment and then three-fourths of the states ratify it, or the process can start in the states themselves, with two-thirds of the states calling for a constitutional convention which could then propose amendments that would in turn have to be ratified by three-fourths of the states. There's a reason the founders made this a difficult process: to make sure it was done only in cases so clear cut that the solution would gain the approval of most Americans.

Expanding the Supreme Court through legislative action would subvert that entire process and weaken the rest of the Constitution. It would be particularly pernicious because, while not prohibited by the Constitution, it would severely undermine it.

The Supreme Court is not the only player on the constitutional field. All branches of government as well as lower federal courts have roles to play. But think of the Supreme Court as the goalie—the penultimate backstop (the ultimate backstop consisting of the voters themselves).

On a soccer team, the goalie has a little more power. She's the only one allowed to use her hands. That's because it's her actions that ultimately determine whether a point is made and the state of play changes. Similarly, the Supreme Court is there to decide what the law says when people disagree as to its meaning. If someone is trying to change a precedent, whether it involves religious freedom protections or presidential power or some other issue of the day, the Court is the governmental equivalent of the goalie—given insulation from political.

If we were to suddenly convert the Supreme Court into a political body, the behavior of its members would necessarily change. They would come to understand their duty as going beyond their proper role of interpreting the law, and taking into account the political will of the president and his or her party. It won't be about sticking to the law and Constitution anymore; it will simply be about approving political decisions. That would weaken our constitutional system immediately and further weaken it to such an extreme degree that I'm not sure what that system would look like. We would be in uncharted territory. The Constitution—which has guided us for more than 230 years—may remain in place, but it would quickly become a shadow of its former self. The constitutional era in American history, as we know it, would be finished.

What would come after that may be too dark to comprehend. If people think American politics is polarized now, imagine what it would be like turning the last apolitical branch of government—which throughout our history has been in a position to offset the political passions of the day when they transgress constitutional limits—into just another instrument of partisanship. The fuel thrown onto the fire would launch flames to heights we dare not imagine.

As our country faces a crucial test, a challenge to the constitutional order not seen in more than a generation, Americans must ask themselves: Are we ready to start down the road to a post-constitutional republic? Is cramming in more justices to push through today's left-wing priorities really worth it—even to Democrats—if we fully consider the consequences?

Americans have stood up before to stop bad ideas whose time had not and should never come. Those of us who want to save the Constitution—especially those who live in states and congressional districts that are (or soon could be) represented by Democrats open to Court packing—have an especially important job to do in the next two election cycles, and in every subsequent election cycle until the idea of packing the Supreme Court has appropriately and permanently been deemed politically toxic. Let me speak with unmistakable clarity here: it's not only those who have expressed sympathy toward Court packing who must be deemed permanently unfit for office, but also any politician lacking the courage to say so.

As I write this, it occurs to me that proponents of Court packing are already planning to use Republican opposition to it to shame Republicans at some future point when, after a Court-packing effort has (heaven forbid) succeeded,

Republicans win enough elections to reciprocate, perhaps increasing the number of seats from 13 to 17. The virtual certainty of that ugly outcome, and the perpetual escalation that would follow, should be reason alone to stop this madness now, before it's too late.

Our institutions and our Constitution are facing an existential threat, but it's not too late to stop it. It's not too late to save nine.

ACKNOWLEDGMENTS

This was a different kind of book for me to write, but I've thoroughly enjoyed the process, and I'm grateful for the guidance and enthusiasm of my editor, Alex Pappas, and his colleagues at Center Street. My longtime agents at Javelin—Keith Urbahn, Matt Latimer, and Dylan Colligan—provided the sterling all-around support that has made us a great team over many books and many years. Sean McGowan contributed valuable research and editorial assistance. My wife, Sharon, helped shape my ideas, and the love and support from her and our children has been constant throughout the process. But this book would not exist at all if it weren't for the many people who helped acquaint me with the Supreme Court over the course of my life—from my parents, Rex and Janet, to Justice Alito, to my brother, Tom.

INTRODUCTION

1. Darragh Roche, "Joe Biden Once Called Court-Packing 'Bonehead Idea': 'Terrible, Terrible Mistake'," *Newsweek*, April 15, 2021, https://www.newsweek.com/joe-biden-once-called-court-packing-bonehead-idea-terrible-terrible-mistake-1583763.

2. Robert Barnes and Ann E. Marimow, "Justice Breyer Warns Proponents of Packing Supreme Court to 'Think Long and Hard' about the Risks," *The Washington Post*, April 7, 2021, https://www.washingtonpost.com/politics/courts_law/justice-breyer-says-expanding-the-supreme-court-will-erode-trust/2021/04/06/cabc95c4-9730-11eb-a6d0-13d207aadb78_story.html.

3. Callie Patteson, "White House's Klain Leaked Breyer Retirement News: Dem Sen. Durbin," *New York Post*, February 1, 2022, https://nypost.com/2022/02/01/white-houses-klain-leaked-breyer-retirement-news-dem-sen-durbin/.

4. Mondaire Jones, "Expand the Supreme Court," April 15, 2021. https://www.facebook.com/MondaireJonesNY17/videos/167035248623033/.

5. Elizabeth Warren, "Expand the Supreme Court," *The Boston Globe*, December 15, 2021, https://www.bostonglobe.com/2021/12/15/opinion/expand-supreme-court/.

6. Tal Axelrod, "Democrats Roll Out Legislation to Expand Supreme Court," The Hill, April 15, 2021, https://thehill.com/homenews/house/548459-democrats-roll-out-legislation-to-expand-supreme-court.

7. Seung Min Kim, "More Democratic Senators Are Willing to Weigh Changes to Supreme Court," *The Washington Post*, December 2, 2021, https://www.washingtonpost.com/politics/senators -overhaul-supreme-court/2021/12/02/efee5458-5374-11ec-8927 -c396fa861a71_story.html.

8. Harvard Law School, "The 2015 Scalia Lectur: A Dialogue with Justice Elena Kagan on the Reading of Statutes," YouTube video, 1:01:12, November 25, 2015, https://www.youtube.com/watch?v =dpEtszFToTg.

CHAPTER ONE

1. Art Pine, "Carter Unveils Plan to Fight Inflation," *The Washington Post*, March 15, 1980, https://www.washingtonpost.com /archive/politics/1980/03/15/carter-unveils-plan-to-fight-inflation /e4ec33d5-0060-4aa7-b7eb-b29770cd0434/.

2. Quoted in Rick Perlstein, *Reaganland: America's Right Turn 1976–1980* (New York: Simon & Schuster, 2020), 446.

3. Ronald Reagan, "Labor Day Speech at Liberty State Park, Jersey City, New Jersey," September 1, 1980. https://www.reaganlibrary.gov/archives /speech/labor-day-speech-liberty-state-park-jersey-city-new-jersey.

4. *Trop* v. *Dulles*, 356 U.S. 86 (1958). https://www.law.cornell.edu /supremecourt/text/356/86.

5. Nick Niedzwiadek, "Poll: Public Opinion of Supreme Court Sags over Past Year," Politico, August 4, 2021, https://www .politico.com/news/2021/08/04/poll-public-opinion-of-supreme -court-sags-over-past-year-502309.

6. Burgess Everett and Marianne Levine, "'Your Credibility... Will Die in This Room'," Politico, October 15, 2020, https://www .politico.com/news/2020/10/15/democrats-supreme-court-retaliation -429655.

7. Linda Greenhouse, "The Supreme Court, Weaponized," *The New York Times*, December 16, 2021, https://www.nytimes.com/2021/12/16/opinion/supreme-court-trump.html?searchResultPosition=1.

8. *The Federalist Papers*, no. 78 (Alexander Hamilton). Library of Congress, accessed January 11, 2022, https://guides.loc.gov/federalist-papers/text-71-80.

9. https://www.washingtonpost.com/news/posteverything/wp/2018/06/28/those-5-4-decisions-on-the-supreme-court-9-0-is-far-more-common/.

10. https://abcnews.go.com/Politics/supreme-court-defies-critics-wave-unanimous-decisions/story?id=78463255.

11. Katie Glueck, "Scalia: The Constitution Is 'Dead'," Politico, January 29, 2013, https://www.politico.com/story/2013/01/scalia-the-constitution-is-dead-086853.

12. Lee Davidson, "Supreme Court Justices Pay Tribute to the Late Rex Lee," *BYU Magazine*, Fall 1996 issue, https://magazine.byu.edu/article/supreme-court-justices-pay-tribute-to-the-late-rex-e-lee/.

CHAPTER TWO

1. Robert McCloskey, *The American Supreme Court* (Chicago: University of Chicago Press, 1960), 19.

2. Quoted in Ron Chernow, *Washington: A Life* (New York: Penguin, 2010), 601.

3. Ibid, 602.

4. "The Court as an Institution," Supreme Court of the United States, https://www.supremecourt.gov/about/institution.aspx.

5. Chernow, *Washington*, 458.

6. https://founders.archives.gov/documents/Adams/99-02-02-4745.

7. McCloskey, *American Supreme Court*, 20.

8. Ron Chernow, *Alexander Hamilton* (New York: Penguin, 2004), 648.

9. Richard A. Samuelson, "The Midnight Appointments," White House Historical Association, *White House History* no. 7, Spring 2000. https://www.whitehousehistory.org /the-midnight-appointments.

10. Chief Justice William Rehnquist, remarks to the Federal Judges Association, May 8, 2001. https://www.supremecourt.gov /publicinfo/speeches/sp_05-08-01.html.

11. Alexander Hamilton, "The Examination Number XIV," March 2, 1802, https://founders.archives.gov/documents/Hamilton /01-25-02-0298.

12. Chernow, *Alexander Hamilton*, 342.

13. Dred Scott v. Sandford, 60 U.S. 393 (1856), https://supreme .justia.com/cases/federal/us/60/393/.

14. https://chroniclingamerica.loc.gov/lccn/sn83016751/1862 -01-03/ed-1/seq-1/#date1=1862&index=0&rows=20&words=last +power+Southern+stronghold&searchType=basic&sequence =0&state=&date2=1863&proxtext=last+stronghold+southern +power&y=23&x=20&dateFilterType=yearRange&page=1.

CHAPTER THREE

1. Keith E. Whittington, "Congress Before the Lochner Court," Boston University Law Review, 85: 821, 2005. https://scholar .princeton.edu/sites/default/files/Congress_Lochner_Court_0.pdf.

2. Robert McCloskey, *The American Supreme Court* (Chicago: University of Chicago Press, 1960), 101.

3. A. Scott Berg, *Wilson* (New York: Berkely Books, 2013), 39.

4. Woodrow Wilson and Ronald J. Pestritto, *The Essential Political Writings of Woodrow Wilson* (Lanham: Lexington Books, 2005), 240.

5. Doris Kearns Goodwin, *The Bully Pulpit: Theodore Roosevelt, William Howard Taft, and the Golden Age of Journalism* (New York: Simon & Schuster, 2013), 15.

6. Wilson and Pestritto, *Writings of Woodrow Wilson*, 121.

7. Noah Feldman, *Scorpions: The Battles and Triumphs of FDR's Great Supreme Court Justices* (New York: Twelve, 2010).

8. Feldman, *Scorpions*, 39.

9. Quoted in Jeffrey Toobin, *The Nine: Inside the Secret World of the Supreme Court* (New York: Anchor, 2008), 1.

10. "Building History," Supreme Court of the United States, https://www.supremecourt.gov/about/buildinghistory.aspx.

CHAPTER FOUR

1. 1936 Electoral College Results, National Archives, https://www.archives.gov/electoral-college/1936#certificates.

2. Charles Evans Hughes, *The Autobiographical Notes of Charles Evans Hughes* (Massachusetts: Harvard University Press, 1973), xi.

3. https://constitutioncenter.org/blog/when-fdrs-blue-eagle-laid-a-supreme-court-egg.

4. "Seven of 9 Justices Hear Roosevelt," *New York Times*, January 21, 1937, https://timesmachine.nytimes.com/timesmachine/1937/01/21/issue.html?auth=login-email.

5. Jeff Shesol, *Supreme Power: Franklin Roosevelt vs. the Supreme Court* (New York: W. W. Norton, 2010), 33.

6. Ibid.

7. *New York Times*, January 21, 1937, https://timesmachine.nytimes.com/timesmachine/1937/01/21/issue.html.

8. Quoted in Shesol, *Supreme Power*, 46.

9. Quoted in Shesol, *Supreme Power*, 3.

10. *The Federalist Papers*, no. 79 (Alexander Hamilton), The Avalon Project at Yale Law School, https://avalon.law.yale.edu/18th _century/fed79.asp.

11. Shesol, *Supreme Power*, 254.

12. Quoted in Noah Feldman, *Scorpions: The Battles and Triumphs of FDR's Great Supreme Court Justices* (New York: Twelve, 2010), 110.

13. Shesol, *Supreme Power*, 4.

14. Shesol, *Supreme Power*, 4.

15. Ibid.

16. Shesol, *Supreme Power*, 6–7.

17. Shesol, *Supreme Power*, 303.

18. Quoted in Shesol, *Supreme Power*, 303.

19. Feldman, *Scorpions*, 109.

CHAPTER FIVE

1. https://www.bbc.com/news/newsbeat-54262657.

2. Quoted in Noah Feldman, *Scorpions: The Battles and Triumphs of FDR's Great Supreme Court Justices* (New York: Twelve, 2010), 119.

3. Ibid, 118.

4. Quoted in Jeff Shesol, *Supreme Power: Franklin Roosevelt vs. the Supreme Court* (New York: W. W. Norton, 2010), 6.

5. Congressional Record: Proceedings and Debates of the First Session of the Seventy-Fifth Congress of the United States of America, Volume 81, Part 10, May 19, 1937 to August 21, 1937 (Washington: United States Government Printing Office, 1937), 1801.

CHAPTER SIX

1. Composition and Jurisdiction of the Supreme Court: Hearing Before a Subcommittee of the Committee on the Judiciary United States Senate, Eighty-Third Congress, Second Session on S.J. Res.

44, January 29, 1954 (Washington: United States Government Printing Office, 1954), 3.

2. "Roberts Fears 'Packing'; Former Justice Supports Plan to Safeguard High Court," *The New York Times*, January 30, 1954.

3. Noah Feldman, *Scorpions: The Battles and Triumphs of FDR's Great Supreme Court Justices* (New York: Twelve, 2010), 274.

4. Composition and Jurisdiction of the Supreme Court.

5. "Roberts Fears."

6. Quoted in James Bryce, *The American Commonwealth*, with an introduction by Gary L. McDowell, 2 vols (Indianapolis: Liberty Fund, 1995).

7. Bryce, *American Commonwealth*.

8. Quoted in Jim Newton, *Justice for All: Earl Warren and the Nation He Made* (New York: Riverhead Hardcover, 2006).

9. Brown v. Board of Education, 347 U.S. 483 (1954), https://www.law.cornell.edu/supremecourt/text/347/483%26gt.

10. Newton, *Justice for All*.

11. Alden Whitman, "For 16 Years, Warren Saw the Constitution as Protector of Rights and Equality," *New York Times*, July 10, 1974.

12. Richard Nixon, Draft of "The New Court," October 23, 1968, Richard Nixon Presidential Library and Museum. https://www.nixonlibrary.gov/news/nixon-and-supreme-court.

CHAPTER SEVEN

1. Nina Totenberg, "Justices Ginsburg and Scalia: A Perfect Match Except for Their Views on the Law," NPR, February 13, 2015, https://www.npr.org/sections/thetwo-way/2015/02/13/386085342/justice-ginsberg-admits-to-being-tipsy-during-state-of-the-union-nap.

2. Dylan Matthews, "Court-Packing, Democrats' Nuclear Option for the Supreme Court, Explained," *Vox*, September 22, 2020, https://www.vox.com/2018/7/2/17513520/court-packing-explained-fdr-roosevelt-new-deal-democrats-supreme-court.

3. Adam Edelman, "Biden Says He Won't Divulge Position on Court Packing Until after Election," NBC News, October 8, 2020, https://www.nbcnews.com/politics/2020-election/biden-says-he-won-t-divulge-position-court-packing-until-n1242658.

4. Darragh Roche, "Joe Biden Once Called Court-Packing 'Bonehead Idea': 'Terrible, Terrible Mistake'," *Newsweek*, April 15, 2021, https://www.newsweek.com/joe-biden-once-called-court-packing-bonehead-idea-terrible-terrible-mistake-1583763.

5. Laurence Tribe, *God Save This Honorable Court* (New York: Random House, 1985).

6. Barbara Sprunt, "Biden Says He's 'Not a Fan' of Expanding the Supreme Court," NPR, October 13, 2020, https://www.npr.org/2020/10/13/923213582/biden-says-hes-not-a-fan-of-expanding-the-supreme-court.

7. Julian E. Zelizer, "Packing the Supreme Court Is a Terrible Idea," *The New York Times*, October 15, 2018, https://www.nytimes.com/2018/10/15/opinion/supreme-court-packing-democrats-.html.

8. Adam Liptak, "The Precedent, and Perils, of Court Packing," *The New York Times*, October 12, 2020, https://www.nytimes.com/2020/10/12/us/supreme-court-packing.html.

9. "President Biden to Sign Executive Order Creating the Presidential Commission on the Supreme Court of the United States," The White House, April 9, 2021. https://www.whitehouse.gov/briefing-room/statements-releases/2021/04/09/president-biden-to-sign-executive-order-creating-the-presidential-commission-on-the-supreme-court-of-the-united-states/.

10. John Fritze, "Biden's Supreme Court Commission 'Divided' on Adding Justices but Warns of 'Considerable' Risk," *USA Today*, October 14, 2021, https://www.usatoday.com/story/news/politics/2021/10/14/biden-commission-weighs-supreme-court-packing-draft-report/8444099002/.

11. Lia Eustachewich, "Democrats Unveil Plan to Pack Supreme Court with 13 Justices," *New York Post*, April 15, 2021, https://nypost.com/2021/04/15/democrats-unveil-plan-to-pack-supreme-court-with-13-justices/.

12. Lisa Hagen, "Democrats Introduce Bill to Expand the Supreme Court but Pelosi Cool to the Idea," *U.S. News & World Report*, April 15, 2021, https://www.usnews.com/news/politics/articles/2021-04-15/democrats-introduce-bill-to-expand-the-supreme-court-but-pelosi-cool-to-the-idea.

13. Aaron Blake, "Biden's Supreme Court Commission Successfully Removes Pie from Sky," *The Washington Post*, October 15, 2021, https://www.washingtonpost.com/politics/2021/10/15/bidens-supreme-court-commission-successfully-removes-pie-sky/.

CHAPTER EIGHT

1. Oral Arguments 08-205, *Citizens United v. Federal Election Commission*, Supreme Court of the United States, March 24, 2009. https://www.supremecourt.gov/oral_arguments/argument_transcripts/2008/08-205.pdf.

2. Ibid.

3. David N. Bossie, "Op-Ed: I'm Responsible for Citizens United. I'm Not Sorry," *Los Angeles Times*, March 1, 2016, https://www.latimes.com/opinion/op-ed/la-oe-0301-bossie-citizens-united-20160226-story.html.

4. Jeffrey Toobin, *The Oath* (New York: Anchor, 2013), 166.

5. Alan Silverleib, "Gloves Come Off after Obama Rips Supreme Court Ruling," CNN, January 28, 2010, https://www.cnn.com/2010/POLITICS/01/28/alito.obama.sotu/index.html.

6. Bill Allison, "Daily Disclosures," Sunlight Foundation, October 18, 2010. https://sunlightfoundation.com/2010/10/18/daily-disclosures-10/.

7. Jane Mayer, Dark Money: The Hidden History of the Billionaires behind the Rise of the Radical Right (New York: Anchor, 2017).

8. Joseph Biden and Michael Carpenter, "Foreign Dark Money Is Threatening American Democracy," *Politico Magazine*, November 27, 2018, https://www.politico.com/magazine/story/2018/11/27/foreign-dark-money-joe-biden-222690/.

9. Ibid.

10. Gideon Resnick and Maxwell Tani, "How Hillary Clinton's Press Secretary Self-Radicalized and Became a Resistance Leader," *Daily Beast*, May 16, 2019, https://www.thedailybeast.com/how-brian-fallon-hillary-clintons-press-secretary-self-radicalized-and-became-a-resistance-leader.

11. Mark Sherman, "New campaign seeks support for expanded Supreme Court," Associated Press, October 16, 2018. https://www.boston.com/news/politics/2018/10/16/new-campaign-seeks-support-for-expanded-supreme-court/.

12. Michael Scherer, "'Court packing' ideas get attention from Democrats," *The Washington Post*, March 11, 2019. https://www.washingtonpost.com/politics/court-packing-ideas-get-attention-from-democrats/2019/03/10/d05e549e-41c0-11e9-a0d3-1210e58a94cf_story.html.

13. Ibid.

14. Joe Schoffstall, "Liberal Dark Money Groups Drive Efforts to Pack the Supreme Court," Fox News, April 21, 2021, https://www.foxnews.com/politics/liberal-dark-money-groups-pack-supreme-court.

15. Ibid.

16. Demand Justice, accessed December 1, 2021, https://demand-justice.org.

17. Ian Prasad Philbrick, "'We May Not Have a Full Two Years': Democrats' Plans Hinge on Good Health," *The New York Times*, May 10, 2021, https://www.nytimes.com/2021/05/10/upshot/democrats-agenda-hinges-health.html.

18. Sherman, "'Court packing' ideas get attention from Democrats."

19. Joseph Bernstein, "Why Is a Top Harvard Law Professor Sharing Anti-Trump Conspiracy Theories?" BuzzFeed News, May 11, 2017. https://www.buzzfeednews.com/article/josephbernstein/larry-tribe-why.

20. Kermit Roosevelt III, "I spent 7 Months Studying Supreme Court Reform. We Need to Pack the Court Now," *Time Magazine*, December 10, 2021, https://time.com/6127193/supreme-court-reform-expansion/.

21. "In Op-Ed, Senator Warren Calls for Supreme Court Expansion to Protect Democracy and Restore Independent Judiciary," Office of Sen. Elizabeth Warren, December 15, 2021. https://www.warren.senate.gov/newsroom/press-releases/in-op-ed-senator-warren-calls-for-supreme-court-expansion-to-protect-democracy-and-restore-independent-judiciary.

CHAPTER NINE

1. Caroline Kitchener and Ellie Silverman, "Protestors at Supreme Court Square Off over abortion," *The Washington Post*, December 1, 2021, https://www.washingtonpost.com/dc-md-va/2021/12/01/abortion-protest-supreme-court-arguments/.

2. Oral Arguments 19-1392, *Dobbs* v. *Jackson Women's Health*, Supreme Court of the United States, December 1, 2021. https://www.supremecourt.gov/oral_arguments/argument_transcripts/2021/19-1392_4425.pdf.

3. Emily Bazelon, "The Place of Women on the Court," *The New York Times Magazine*, July 7, 2009. https://www.nytimes.com/2009/07/12/magazine/12ginsburg-t.html.

4. "In Her Own Words: Ruth Bader Ginsburg," *The New York Times*, June 15, 1993. https://www.nytimes.com/1993/06/15/us/the-supreme-court-in-her-own-words-ruth-bader-ginsburg.html.

5. Ibid.

6. Andrew Mark Miller, "Sotomayor Compares Fetus to Brain Dead Person, Says Fetal Movement Doesn't Prove Consciousness," Fox News, December 1, 2021, https://www.foxnews.com/politics/sotomayor-compares-fetus-brain-dead-person-fetal-movement-consciousness.

7. Krishnadev Calamur and Nina Totenberg, "Breyer Warns against Remaking the Court: 'What Goes Around Comes Around'," NPR, September 10, 2021, https://www.npr.org/2021/09/10/1035592358/breyer-warns-against-remaking-the-court-what-goes-around-comes-around.

8. Carl Hulse, "Abortion Decision Could Spill into Midterm Elections," *The New York Times*, December 1, 2021, https://www.nytimes.com/2021/12/01/us/abortion-midterm-elections-supreme-court.html.

9. Antonin Scalia, *The Essential Scalia* (New York: Crown Forum, 2020), 36.

MIKE LEE is a United States senator from Utah and a member of the Senate Judiciary Committee. Lee's interest in the Supreme Court began when he was only ten years old and his father, the late Rex Edwin Lee—then serving as President Ronald Reagan's solicitor general—started bringing the future senator with him when he argued cases before the Court. After graduating from law school, Lee served as a law clerk to Associate Justice Samuel A. Alito, Jr., first on the U.S. Court of Appeals for the Third Circuit, and then on the Supreme Court. Before entering politics, Lee served as an assistant U.S. attorney and later as general counsel to Utah Governor Jon M. Huntsman, Jr. During his years in private practice, he specialized in appellate and Supreme Court litigation. Lee, a *New York Times* bestselling author, has written several books on American political and legal history.